HV4708 .A566 2011

Animal welfare

GLOBALVIEWPOINTS

Animal Welfare

DISCARDED

Other Books of Related Interest:

At Issue Series
Biodiversity

Current Controversies Series
Factory Farming
Vegetarianism

Global Viewpoints Series
Food

Introducing Issues with Opposing Viewpoints Series
Animal Rights
Organic Food and Farming

Issues on Trial Series
Animal Welfare

Issues That Concern You Series
Endangered Species

Social Issues in Literature
Bioethics in Mary Shelley's *Frankenstein*

GLOBALVIEWPOINTS

Animal Welfare

Christina Fisanick, Book Editor

GREENHAVEN PRESS
A part of Gale, Cengage Learning

GALE
CENGAGE Learning

Detroit • New York • San Francisco • New Haven, Conn • Waterville, Maine • London

GALE
CENGAGE Learning

Christine Nasso, *Publisher*
Elizabeth Des Chenes, *Managing Editor*

© 2011 Greenhaven Press, a part of Gale, Cengage Learning

Gale and Greenhaven Press are registered trademarks used herein under license.

For more information, contact:
Greenhaven Press
27500 Drake Rd.
Farmington Hills, MI 48331-3535
Or you can visit our Internet site at gale.cengage.com

For product information and technology assistance, contact us at

Gale Customer Support, 1-800-877-4253
For permission to use material from this text or product, submit all requests online at
www.cengage.com/permissions

Further permissions questions can be emailed to permissionrequest@cengage.com

Articles in Greenhaven Press anthologies are often edited for length to meet page requirements. In addition, original titles of these works are changed to clearly present the main thesis and to explicitly indicate the author's opinion. Every effort is made to ensure that Greenhaven Press accurately reflects the original intent of the authors. Every effort has been made to trace the owners of copyrighted material.

Cover image © Karen Kasmauski/Corbis.

LIBRARY OF CONGRESS CATALOGING-IN-PUBLICATION DATA

Animal welfare / Christina Fisanick, book editor.
    p. cm. -- (Global viewpoints)
    Includes bibliographical references and index.
    ISBN 978-0-7377-5187-1 (hbk.) -- ISBN 978-0-7377-5188-8 (pbk.)
    1. Animal welfare--Juvenile literature. I. Fisanick, Christina.
    HV4708.A566 2011
    179'.3--dc22
                                     2010039548

Printed in the United States of America
1 2 3 4 5   15 14 13 12 11

ED066

Contents

Chapter 2: Animal Welfare and Global Biomedical Research

Chapter 3: The World Food Industry and Animal Welfare

Chapter 4: Animal Ownership and Animal Welfare Around the World

Foreword

"The problems of all of humanity can only be solved by all of humanity."
—Swiss author Friedrich Dürrenmatt

Global interdependence has become an undeniable reality. Mass media and technology have increased worldwide access to information and created a society of global citizens. Understanding and navigating this global community is a challenge, requiring a high degree of information literacy and a new level of learning sophistication.

Building on the success of its flagship series, *Opposing Viewpoints*, Greenhaven Press has created the *Global Viewpoints* series to examine a broad range of current, often controversial topics of worldwide importance from a variety of international perspectives. Providing students and other readers with the information they need to explore global connections and think critically about worldwide implications, each *Global Viewpoints* volume offers a panoramic view of a topic of widespread significance.

Drugs, famine, immigration—a broad, international treatment is essential to do justice to social, environmental, health, and political issues such as these. Junior high, high school, and early college students, as well as general readers, can all use *Global Viewpoints* anthologies to discern the complexities relating to each issue. Readers will be able to examine unique national perspectives while, at the same time, appreciating the interconnectedness that global priorities bring to all nations and cultures.

Material in each volume is selected from a diverse range of sources, including journals, magazines, newspapers, nonfiction books, speeches, government documents, pamphlets, organization newsletters, and position papers. *Global Viewpoints* is truly global, with material drawn primarily from international sources available in English and secondarily from U.S. sources with extensive international coverage.

Features of each volume in the *Global Viewpoints* series include:

- An **annotated table of contents** that provides a brief summary of each essay in the volume, including the name of the country or area covered in the essay.

- An **introduction** specific to the volume topic.

- A **world map** to help readers locate the countries or areas covered in the essays.

- For each viewpoint, an **introduction** that contains notes about the author and source of the viewpoint explains why material from the specific country is being presented, summarizes the main points of the viewpoint, and offers three **guided reading questions** to aid in understanding and comprehension.

- **For further discussion** questions that promote critical thinking by asking the reader to compare and contrast aspects of the viewpoints or draw conclusions about perspectives and arguments.

- A worldwide list of **organizations to contact** for readers seeking additional information.

- A **periodical bibliography** for each chapter and a **bibliography of books** on the volume topic to aid in further research.

- A comprehensive **subject index** to offer access to people, places, events, and subjects cited in the text, with the countries covered in the viewpoints highlighted.

Global Viewpoints is designed for a broad spectrum of readers who want to learn more about current events, history, political science, government, international relations, economics, environmental science, world cultures, and sociology—students doing research for class assignments or debates, teachers and faculty seeking to supplement course materials, and others wanting to understand current issues better. By presenting how people in various countries perceive the root causes, current consequences, and proposed solutions to worldwide challenges, *Global Viewpoints* volumes offer readers opportunities to enhance their global awareness and their knowledge of cultures worldwide.

Introduction

"There is a fundamental difference be-
tween cows and screwdrivers. Cows feel
pain and screwdrivers do not."

—Temple Grandin,
"Animals Are Not Things:
A View on Animal Welfare Based
on Neurological Complexity," 2002

The relationship between humans and animals spans thousands of years. In many ways, human civilization could not exist as it does today without animals, which have been used for work, food, clothing, protection, and companionship, among other uses. Given this unique relationship, concern for the well-being of animals is beneficial not only for people who depend on them but also for the animals themselves. It is no surprise, then, that even ancient philosophers debated the rights of animals, and this debate is more important today as the need for animals grows as the human population increases.

Proclamations about the rights of animals can be traced to the earliest of recorded texts. In *The Lankavatara Sutra* (circa 599–510 BCE), Buddha, Buddhism's prophet and founder, deplored the consumption of animals. He wrote, "cherish the thought of kinship with [living beings] and refrain from meat-eating. . . . Meat-eating I have not permitted to anyone, I do not permit, I will not permit." Later, this view is challenged by early Christian teachings. In Genesis 1:20–28, God gave Adam "dominion over the fish of the sea, and over the fowl of the air, and over the cattle, and over all the earth, and over every creeping thing that creepeth upon the earth." Although contemporary scholars and animal rights activists argue whether this statement indicates that God grants ownership of animals to human beings, this particular passage is frequently cited as an indictment for people to freely partake of animal flesh.

Such opposing views of the rights of animals continued to be expressed through the ages. In the seventeenth century, the debate entered the realm of philosophy and the beginning of the scientific revolution. René Descartes, French mathematician and philosopher, declared in *Discourse on the Method* in 1637 that animals are not sentient beings. They have no awareness or feelings. Therefore, human beings have the right to use animals as they do any other product in the environment. Not everyone agreed with Descartes. Political leader Thomas Wentworth is known to have passed the first animal rights law in the English-speaking world when in Ireland in 1635 he decreed it unlawful to pull the wool off sheep and to hook plows up to horses' tails. Wentworth's proclamation was followed by similar legislation in the Massachusetts Bay Colony in 1641. According to the colony's constitution, *The Body of Liberties*, "No man shall exercise any Tirrany or Crueltie toward any bruite Creature which are usuallie kept for man's use."

Interest in animal welfare continued to grow, which led to the passage of Martin's Act in 1822. Colonel Richard Martin of Ireland proposed "An Act to Prevent the Cruel and Improper Treatment of Cattle" to Parliament. At first, the other members dismissed Martin's concern, convinced that animals, especially cattle, had no right to protection under the law. Nonetheless, Martin pushed his bill through, which made it illegal to "beat, abuse, or ill-treat any horse, mare, gelding, mule, ass, ox, cow, heifer, steer, sheep or other cattle." Fearing that the law would not be enforced, concerned members of Parliament and other citizens joined together to form the Royal Society for the Prevention of Cruelty to Animals (RSPCA) in 1840, which was supported by Queen Victoria of England, who was against animal experimentation. The American Society for the Prevention of Cruelty to Animals (ASPCA) was founded not long after, in 1866.

The twentieth century ushered in a new wave of animal rights supporters as the scientific revolution spread throughout the world, and animals were increasingly used in experiments. Surprisingly, the Nazi Party of Germany passed some of the most comprehensive legislation in favor of the rights of animals in the world. Soon after the Nazis took power in 1933, they passed what was known as *Tierschutzgesetz*, a set of laws that forbade animal cruelty throughout the Third Reich. Shortly after, Nazi leader Adolf Hitler banned hunting and proclaimed the correct way to shoe horses, boil crustaceans, and treat animals in general. He was well known as a vegetarian and lover of dogs. Unfortunately, as Trinity College history professor Kathleen Kete remarked in a 2001 interview with journalist Sina Najafi in *Cabinet*, "Humans as a species lost their special—sacrosanct—status and a new hierarchy of being was established whereby some 'races' of animals lay above some 'races' of humans. Wolves, eagles, and Teutonic pigs ('despised by the Jews') are near the top of the Nazi chain-of-being. Jews and rats are on the bottom." In other words, according to Kete, Nazi animal protection laws might have been passed more to attack Jewish beliefs and practices than to support the well-being of animals. In fact, in the latter days of the regime, Nazis freely experimented on animals to corroborate the tests they performed on Jews and other "undesirable" people.

The fall of Nazi Germany ushered in a dismantling of the most extreme of those animal rights laws, but the concern for animals across the globe continued to build. In 1959 W.M.S. Russell and R.L. Burch wrote "The Removal of Inhumanity: The Three R's", a groundbreaking work that provoked a discussion and then a movement of alternatives for animal testing. The three Rs in regard to animal testing are replacement, reduction, and refinement. In short, Russell and Burch recommended that researchers replace animals with nonanimal test sites, reduce the number of animal used, and refine research methods to make experiments more useful and less painful to animals used. Since the publication of the three Rs, animal rights advocates have added to and amended the recommendations, and alternative methods to animal testing have been developed, including using computer programs to simulate human reactions.

In 1975 Australian philosopher Peter Singer published *Animal Liberation,* a book that is considered the bible of the modern animal liberation movement. Singer made the claim that the issue was not about whether animals had rights but about their ability to feel pain. He popularized the term "speciesism," which was originally coined by Richard Ryder, a British philosopher opposed to animal experimentation. In both of their views, speciesism, or the discrimination of a being based on its species, is wrong and is not an excuse for the exploitation of animals or people.

The end of the twentieth century witnessed an enormous growth in the animal liberation movement with the founding of many animal rights organizations and campaigns for the protection of animal rights throughout the world. One of the most successful campaigns was led by Henry Spira and Animal Rights International (ARI), the group he founded in 1974. In 1980 Spira and ARI took out full-page newspaper ads to convince the cosmetics company Revlon to stop using the Draize test, which involved dripping substances into animals' eyes to determine their safety for use on humans. The *New York Times* ad featured a rabbit with wounded eyes and the question, "How many rabbits does Revlon blind for beauty's sake?" According to "Pressuring Perdue," an article by Barnaby J. Feder that appeared in the November 26, 1989, issue of the *New York Times,* Revlon and a number of other cosmetics companies made significant donations to ARI, which led to the formation of the Center for Alternatives to Animal Testing.

Significant progress for animal rights has been made in the first part of the twenty-first century. Animal rights organizations have grown in membership, and more people including scientists have pushed for better treatment of animals. For example, recent studies reported in the United Kingdom's *Sunday Times* reveal that dolphins are second only to humans in terms of intelligence and brain size. In a January 3, 2010, article by Jonathan Leake, Emory University zoologist Lori Marino noted that her research confirmed that dolphins should be protected against harm because they are intelligent, have a strong sense of self, and can think about the future. Later in the article, Thomas White of Loyola Marymount University added, "The scientific research ... suggests that dolphins are 'nonhuman persons' who qualify for moral standing as individuals."

In 2008 the Food and Drug Administration of the United States declared meat from cloned animals safe for human consumption. This declaration, along with similar statements around the world, has ushered in a new age of animal welfare and has further complicated the human-animal relationship. The authors in *Global Viewpoints: Animal Welfare* debate current views on the subject in the following chapters: Cultural and Religious Views on Animal Rights, Animal Welfare and Global Biomedical Research, The World Food Industry and Animal Welfare, and Animal Ownership and Animal Welfare Around the World. The viewpoints within reveal the constant debate about how humans and animals struggle to co-exist on a planet with ever-increasing demands on its resources.

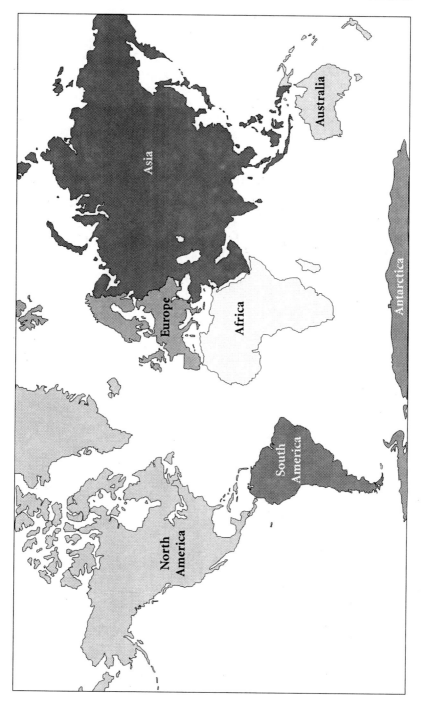

Cultural and Religious Views on Animal Rights

Islamic Beliefs Require That Animals Be Treated Humanely

PR Newswire

PR Newswire delivers news and multimedia content for corporations, public relations firms, and nongovernmental organizations according to the "simultaneous disclosure" standard required by financial markets and regulatory agencies. The Council on American-Islamic Relations (CAIR) is America's largest Islamic civil liberties group. In the following viewpoint, the author opposes the claim that Islam "encourages killing." Using the Quran, the Muslim holy book, and other religious documents, the author shows that Islam requires humans to respect and care for animals.

As you read, consider the following questions:

1. What situation in Iraq was the occasion for Paul Harvey to make the claim that Islam "encourages killing"?
2. According to CAIR, what did Muhammad say happened to the woman with the cat?
3. According to CAIR, what did Muhammad say was the reward for the man who helped a thirsty animal?

The Council on American-Islamic Relations (CAIR) is calling for an on-air apology from syndicated radio commentator Paul Harvey who said on his Thursday [December 2003] program that Islam "encourages killing."

Harvey, who has 24 million weekly listeners on some 1,600 radio stations in this country and around the world, made that claim during his Thursday noon commentary.

In that segment, Harvey described the bloody nature of cockfight gambling in Iraq and said: "Add to the thirst for blood a religion which encourages killing, and it is entirely understandable if Americans came to this bloody party unprepared." . . .

"We had hoped that a respected broadcast professional like Mr. Harvey would not join the growing number of Islamophobic hate-mongers in our society," said CAIR Communications Director Ibrahim Hooper. "He falsely attributes to Islam two things that are specifically prohibited by our faith, murder and cruelty to animals." (Islam also prohibits gambling.)

Hooper quoted the Prophet Muhammad, who said one of the "biggest of (the great sins)" is "to murder a human being." (Sahih al-Bukhari, 9:10) He also cited the Quran, Islam's revealed text, which states that when someone takes another's life, "it would be as if he slew all mankind." (Quran, 5:32)

On animal cruelty, the Prophet said: "A woman was punished [by God] because of a cat. She had neither provided it with food nor drink, nor set it free so that it might eat the creatures of the earth." (Sahih Muslim, Hadith 1047)

[Muhammad] prohibited capturing young birds because of the distress caused to their mother.

In another tradition related by the Prophet, a man was rewarded by God for helping a thirsty animal. The man, who had just climbed down a well to get water for himself, saw a dog panting and licking mud because of excessive thirst. He went down the well again and filled his shoe with water for the dog. God thanked him for that deed and forgave his sins.

After relating that story, the Prophet was asked: "Is there a reward for us in serving animals?" He replied: "Yes, there is a reward for serving any (living being)." (Sahih al-Bukhari, 3:646)

In other Islamic traditions, the Prophet prohibited capturing young birds because of the distress caused to their mother, and rebuked his companions who burnt an ant hill.

Hooper also cited the Quran, which says: "There is no beast that walks on earth and no bird that flies on its two wings that is not [God's] creature . . . Unto their Sustainer shall they [all] be gathered." (Quran, 6:38)

In 1999, Harvey issued an on-air apology to Muslims for remarks suggesting that Islam was a "fraudulent religion." The apology came after hundreds of concerned Muslims called, faxed and e-mailed both Harvey's office and that of ABC Radio Networks, his program's syndicator.

CAIR, America's largest Islamic civil liberties group, is headquartered in Washington, D.C., and has 25 regional offices and chapters nationwide and in Canada.

Cockfighting Remains Legal and Popular in the Dominican Republic

DR1.com

DR1.com is a website devoted to connecting people from the Dominican Republic to their relatives and friends at home and abroad. In the following viewpoint, DR1.com argues that while cockfighting—pitting two roosters against each other usually for money—is seen as violent and inhumane in the Western world, it remains a popular pastime in the Dominican Republic. Owners of fighting cocks spend considerable time and money preparing their fowls for the ring, and spectators number well into the thousands. Although it is currently legal, cockfighting does have its opponents.

As you read, consider the following questions:

1. Where and when do some scholars say that cockfighting got its start?
2. Name at least three countries in which cockfighting remains a popular sport.
3. According to a survey by Mark Feierstein, what percentage of Dominicans do not approve of cockfighting as a sport?

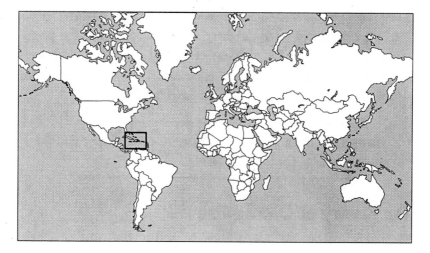

Some define it as a representation of war or the extension of human aggression, complete with its own theatrical components and metaphorical language, while others classify it as vile, sacrificial, archaic and disgusting. Some stand behind the cloak of culture, customs and history to defend its existence and continued practice, while others deem it barbaric, regressive, inhuman and exploitative.

No, this is not boxing or mixed martial arts, it's cockfighting.

The blood sport, which consists of two bred and highly trained roosters pitted against each other in a fight to the death, is a controversial topic. There is no denying the popularity of cockfighting within some strata of Dominican society. Breeders in the DR [Dominican Republic] have become experts in breeding contest-ready game, and they spare no expense in preparing their fowl for competition. In some cases the cocks are treated better than family members, receiving specially prepared meals, vitamins, massages and baths in preparation for what could be very lucrative fights.

Outsiders to the cockfighting "culture" seem either baffled or disgusted by the sport, while insiders accentuate, not the bloodiness of it all, but the beauty and the drama that accompany the fights. Either way, as part of a defined pastime in the DR it is important to understand the factors behind the popularity of cockfighting in this country, why certain measures are taken to maintain its status as a sport, and to determine whether in fact cockfighting is as popular as publicized.

There is no denying the popularity of cockfighting within some strata of Dominican society.

The History of Cockfighting

Cockfighting can be traced back to before the time of Christ with some scholars indicating that the sport had its start in India more than 4,600 years ago. The rooster had long been considered an admirable fowl before its entrance into the fighting arena. The ancient Syrians, for example, worshiped the rooster as a deity. In addition, the ancient Greeks and Romans associated the bird with the gods Apollo, Mercury and Mars.

Approximately 3,000 years ago cockfighting was popular with the Hebrews and Canaanites, and raising gamecocks was considered a skill with a lucrative end. For Egyptians cockfighting was a favored pastime and during the height of Greek civilization, a Greek general, Themistocles, held a cockfight the night before battle to inspire his men through the metaphor of the cockfight.

Persian traders loved to gamble by pitting their fighting birds against each other, and the popularity of the sport even stretched to the Roman Empire. Julius Caesar, the first citizen of Rome to become an aficionado of the sport, brought cockfighting to Rome.

It took a while for the sport to spread, but by the 16th century it was popular in many European countries, especially in England and France. During the reign of King Henry VIII, cockfighting became a national sport. Schools were even founded to teach students the fine points of cockfighting. At its very height of popularity, the sport was popular among the church members with churchyards being used as cockfighting arenas. However, by the 17th century the sport declined in popularity in England and later on Queen Victoria banned cockfighting with a royal decree.

The sport was also very popular in the United States during the 18th and 19th centuries. Presidents like George Washington, Thomas Jefferson, Andrew Jackson and Abraham Lincoln were admirers of the sport and rumor has it that President Lincoln got his nickname "Honest Abe" for his fairness as a judge in cockfights. Overall, it was socially acceptable and encouraged to have gamecocks. The U.S. would eventually become a center for cockfighting activities and events, and the fighting cock almost became the national emblem of the United States, losing by just one vote to the American eagle. However, by the beginning of the Civil War the sport had lost much of its attraction and appeal.

Today, cockfighting is a popular sport in many places around the world including Haiti, Nicaragua, Venezuela, Colombia, France, Mexico, Italy, the Philippines, Peru, Puerto Rico, the Canary Islands, Guam, India and Pakistan.

The History of Cockfights in the Dominican Republic

Not much information exists on how and why cockfighting got to the DR, although some believe that it was brought over by the Spanish, maintaining its popularity during French and Haitian colonial rule. Very little exists in terms of text associated with the sport of cockfighting, with mentions restricted to liner notes and obscure references in certain texts. However, the importance of cocks is highlighted in Dominican history through political references, most notably through the "bolos patas blancas" and "bolos patas prietas" parties, in references to the factions of Horacio Vásquez's "bolo" political movement of the 1910s. The rooster also has a significant place in Dominican history as it was and still is the symbol of the Partido Reformista Social Cristiano (PRSC). The PRSC morphed from the [Rafael] Trujillo-run Partido Dominicano to the PRSC after the dictator's longtime right-hand man, intellectual Joaquín Balaguer, took over the reins of the country in 1966 and governed, officially and extra officially, until his death in 2000.

During this time, the symbol of the rooster gained a special place in the nuances of Dominican cultural identity and came to represent the virtues of the Dominican political spirit, further enamoring the public to this fowl. But social commentators like Gustav Jahoda claim that, "in many cultures, notably hunting-gathering ones, animals are believed to have souls and to be in close partnership with humans," taking the argument a step further and presenting the idea that the ritualistic behavior of the cockfight represents the social dynamic which asserts a male's place in Dominican society. The reason men look to animals to describe themselves is because, according to Jahoda, there is an inherent connection between humans and animals, and thus understanding the affection between man and fowl is more plausible.

In looking at a cockfight, and its prominence as a national sport, one notices how a Dominican male views himself through the lens of the animal. "Like politics on Hispaniola, the cockfight is a male ritual," writes Jahoda. The cockfight, and in turn the rooster, represent the spirit of the Dominican male, and this is why one can argue that cockfighting has carved a special place within the Dominican psyche. According to popular author Michele Wucker,

In the cockfight, man and beast, good and evil, ego and id, the creative power of aroused masculinity and the destructive power of loosened animality fuse in a bloody drama of hatred, cruelty, violence, and death. Emotions are displayed

A Fighting Rooster Is a Human Invention

A good gamecock, like a good roaster, is largely a human invention. Three thousand years ago, Asian cockfighters took the most unfriendly birds on the planet—jungle fowl, *Gallus gallus*—and proceeded to make them even meaner. Over the years, cockfighters crossed them with Himalayan Bankivas for speed and flying kicks, and with Malay birds for stamina and wallop. They taught them to punch and feint and roll. They marched them through gamecock calisthenics, trimmed their wattles and combs, and stuffed red pepper up their anuses. A few thousand generations later, this was the result: two birds programmed to kill each other, each a glimmering alloy of instinct, training, and breeding.

Burkhard Bilger, "Enter the Chicken,"
Harper's Magazine, *March 1, 1999.*

in a cathartic microcosm of human interaction, violence released through the flailing spurs, beaks, and feathers in the ring.

The rooster has come to represent all aspects of daily life in the Dominican Republic, according to Wucker. "The rooster represents politics, home, territory, courtship, healing, sustenance, the passage of time, and brotherhood."

The cockfight, and in turn the rooster, represent the spirit of the Dominican male.

Preparation

Cockfighting can be a very lucrative endeavor, with men spending thousands upon thousands of pesos or dollars on nurturing a prize bird for a fight. Training begins at a very early stage with the owner sparing no expense to guarantee his bird the best chance to be a winner. At times, these birds are treated even better than family members, receiving better care and more attention.

Preparation for a fight begins close to two years before the bird ever steps into the ring. Many fighting birds are hatched from hens with a record of mothering good fighting birds. From birth they are fed a diet of special grains, vitamins and antibiotics. When the bird is fight-ready, professional groomers trim its feathers, the underbelly is shaved and its combs and wattles are surgically removed. Groomers also cut the birds' spurs with a sharp knife before fitting them with spikes. The new spurs can be metal and are used to inflict more pain, which could lead to a bird's death in an even quicker fashion. The spikes are affixed with a few drops of hot wax, and then taped. The owners smooth away any excess wax with wet fingertips, and make sure that the spikes are straight. Before a fight, a licensed fowl inspector uses an acid rinse that changes color when illegal substances are present on the birds' skin. This rinse is necessary in order to detect foreign or illegal substances that could give one fowl an advantage over another. Sometimes owners rub tobacco or other chemicals on the roosters, to make the bird fight harder or to affect the opponent bird.

At times, these birds are treated even better than family members.

The atmosphere at a *gallera*, Spanish for the fighting ring, is what's most interesting. Moments before the fight begins there is silence, with onlookers quieting to see the two "opponents". The birds are brought into the circle. Depending on the gallera you are at, the fighting ring could be a dirt floor or an artificial grass floor, as is the case at Santo Domingo's

Coliseo Gallistico. The Coliseo is a modern building fit for human fights, but its simplicity is a testament to the importance of the sport among some in this society.

Once the matches are set, the fowl handlers drop the two birds into the center of the circle and the fight begins. And this is where the madness starts. This crucial moment is where proponents feel a surge of crude energy and adrenaline and where opponents cringe at the thought of another bird being killed.

The roosters raise their hackles, then peck and circle each other. As they slowly dance around the circle pecking and inflicting damage on each other, hordes of men shout as loud as they can, betting on the bird of their choice. Money changes hands rapidly and one would think they were on the trading floor on Wall Street and not a cock fight in the DR. Bets range from RD$500 [in Dominican currency] to as much as one is willing to take on. In smaller and less organized cockfights, the bets are much smaller. In many cases the bets are never recorded, but are honored by a special understanding between the betters. In these cases a man's honor and ability to live up to his bet is worth his weight in gold.

The atmosphere at a gallera, *Spanish for the fighting ring, is what's most interesting.*

As the fight continues, the brutality becomes more evident. Slowly one of the birds begins to succumb to the slow painful pecks. Sensing close victory, the winning bird continues to pounce as blood begins to squirt and drip out. Feathers are flying and the defeated bird is now one step closer to death.

Opposing Views

There are many arguments that defend the viability and necessity of cockfighting. Among the leading arguments by proponents is that above anything else cockfighting is a cultural phenomenon that must be respected as part of the overall Dominican cultural landscape. Many supporters believe that just as bullfighting is popular in Spain, Colombia or Argentina, cockfighting is a tradition on which many virtues and values are hinged on and thus must be respected, protected and conserved. Supporters will also argue about the historical importance of the rooster, considering that the sport has been around for too long to be abolished. Continued arguments put forward the idea that cockfighting is a money generator which creates and circulates funds for local farmers and businesses. Some say that there are as many as 3,000 galleras in the DR with as many as 24,000 men gaining employment from the sport. Proponents say that cockfighting produces millions of dollars in formal and informal revenues, and it would be an economic and financial blow to surrounding communities if the sport were abolished. Finally, among the most enduring arguments is the one that indicates that roosters are by nature, aggressive animals that will inherently fight at the sight of another rooster, and conventional wisdom would then indicate that if they are already doing it, then how and why stop them from doing so? Finally, some argue that roosters are brainless animals and that this in itself is a justification to allow them to fight to the death.

For every argument that exists in favor of cockfighting, there are just as many condemning the blood sport and that discount all supportive arguments. Opponents are quick to argue that cockfighting, and any blood sport in general, is cruel to animals and should therefore not be practiced. Another viable argument states that as the highest form of intelligence on this planet, we must respect the lives of other animals and that it is our responsibility not to partake in cruelty to animals. Adding to this is the argument that profiting from the cruelty, death or suffering of another animal is unfair and cruel. Opponents also argue that while roosters are hostile, this only occurs in a territorial context and they are not inherently aggressive towards other roosters. One final argument is that although cockfighting is a profitable endeavor, it is not as profitable as some would make it seem and that the abolition of the sport would not be as devastating to the economies of local communities as has been argued.

Some say that there are as many as 3,000 galleras in the DR with as many as 24,000 men gaining employment from the sport.

Interestingly enough, a survey by Mark Feierstein, vice president of [consulting firm] Greenberg Quinlan Rosner showed that 52% of Dominicans disapprove of cockfighting as a sport, including 60% of women and 62% of the affluent, while 40% of Dominicans [in this group] firmly disapprove of the sport. Peripheral arguments include that unlike other violent sports, cockfighting is a fight to the death and has no rules, and for this reason the sport should be banned.

The Sport's Legality

There are a myriad of personal viewpoints that support and oppose this controversial sport, but it seems that cockfighting won't be banned any time soon. Part of cockfighting's strength is its support base, garnering the participation of wealthy and famous Dominicans both in the country and abroad. Many big name politicians are also in favor of the sport. Adding to this is the fact that much of the electorate are fans of the sport, any administration would unlikely alienate that voter base by outlawing a sport that they hold dear. Recently, Sports Minister Felipe Payano assured the DR's cockfighting sector that the government would continue to support the sport. Payano took the time to highlight President Leonel Fernández's efforts to strengthen the cockfighting sector in the DR.

Despite being illegal and looked down upon in the US and Europe, cockfighting is legal and considered part of the DR's cultural heritage, but how long will this fact hold true? Some believe that support for this sport will decline as a product of time and as Dominicans become more educated on the concept of animal rights. As was highlighted in this [viewpoint] there is a growing number of Dominicans who don't support cockfighting, yet it will take time for those voices to shout in unison against the sport. Until then the conversation will rage on as to whether or not to allow cockfighting, with both sides citing the pros and cons. One thing is for sure is that the conversation will not take place at the [*gallera*] Coliseo Gallistico.

The Prohibition of Ritual Animal Slaughter Throughout the World Is Cultural Discrimination

Pablo Lerner and Alfredo Mordechai Rabello

Killing animals without stunning them first, which is a kind of ritual slaughter, is against the law in some countries, but it is required by some religions including Judaism and Islam. In the following viewpoint, Pablo Lerner and Alfredo Mordechai Rabello argue that prohibiting the ritual slaughter of animals is cultural and religious discrimination. Lerner is a senior lecturer at Ramat Gan Law School in Israel, and Rabello is a professor of law at the Hebrew University of Jerusalem and the University of Haifa in Israel.

As you read, consider the following questions:

1. Where can the required techniques for animal slaughtering in Muslim culture be found?

2. What was René Descartes's stance on animal rights?

3. What is the choice theory of rights, according to the viewpoint?

Pablo Lerner and Alfredo Mordechai Rabello, "The Prohibition of Ritual Slaughtering (Kosher Shechita and Halal) and Freedom of Religion of Minorities," *Journal of Law & Religion*, vol. 22, no. 1, 2006–2007, pp. 1, 9–12, 21–26, 31–32. Copyright © 2006–2007 by HAMLINE UNIVERSITY, SCHOOL OF LAW. Reproduced by permission.

The statutory prohibition against ritual slaughter, which does not stun the animal prior to slaughter, as required in most Western nations, poses a significant challenge for the international right to freedom of religion or belief in European nation-states. This prohibition is important not only in Europe, or because of the prohibition itself, but also because it implicates the legal status of two minority religious communities in these nation-states, those of Judaism and Islam. Some animal rights advocates have objected to ritual slaughter without stunning because, in their view, it causes needless suffering by the animal, and they have been successful in getting their views enacted into law in a number of European countries. Indeed, some countries prohibit ritual slaughtering altogether, as we shall discuss below.

This [viewpoint] argues that the right to freedom of religion or belief requires nation-states to respect the rights of religious minorities that engage in ritual slaughter, even if they recognize the importance of avoiding unnecessary suffering of animals. . . .

Jewish and Muslim Laws

Modern attempts to regulate ritual slaughtering of farm animals vary in their understanding of what is entailed in ritual slaughtering. . . .

We define religious or ritual slaughter as a procedure carried out according to rules originating from ancient religious laws. The religious nature of slaughtering relates primarily to Jewish and Muslim slaughter, and as was indicated earlier, kosher and *halal* slaughtering are done without stunning. The relevant precept originates from Scriptures:

> If the place which the Lord thy God shall choose to put His name there be too far from thee, then thou shalt kill of thy herd and of thy flock, which the Lord hath given thee, as I have commanded thee, and thou shalt eat within thy gates, after all the desire of thy soul.

As a matter of fact, Scriptures do not give details of the technique of slaughtering—rather, they are expounded by oral law.

According to the *Halakhah*, the killing of an animal for purposes of eating its meat must be performed by an expert who severs the animal's gullet and windpipe with one slash, after making sure that the knife is sharpened according to *halakhic* specifications. [Moses] Maimonides [a medieval Jewish philosopher] regards these specifications of slaughtering as proof that the law calls for a painless and easy death for the animal.

> [F]or as it has become necessary to eat the flesh of animals, it was intended by the above regulations to ensure an easy death and to effect it by suitable means; whilst decapitation requires a sword or a similar instrument, the shechita can be performed with any instrument; and in order to ensure an easy death our Sages insisted that the knife should be well sharpened.[. . .] Since, therefore, the desire of procuring good food necessitates the slaying of animals, the Law enjoins that the death of the animal should be the easiest. It is not allowed to torment the animal by cutting the throat in a clumsy manner, by pole-axing, or by cutting off a limb whilst the animal is alive.

Although these texts emanate from a time when stunning was not universally practiced, they show a clear animal welfare–oriented approach in Jewish thinking regarding slaughtering.

For Muslims, there are four sources of Muslim law concerning *halal* (permissible meat): the Qur'an, the *hadith*, the *sunnah* and *fiqh*. Islamic rules for slaughtering resemble the Jewish approach in many respects, while differing in others. Apart from the obvious differences in the prescribed prayers (the Hebrew benediction and the Arabic *bismillah Allahu akbar*), there is no requirement that the Muslim slaughterer should be a trained expert. According to some opinions, Muslim law is not as strict with regard to the prohibition of prior stunning as Jewish law. While according to Jewish law stunning may impair the perfection of the animal and not allow the consumer to discern whether it is *trepha*, there are those who claim that the position adopted by Muslim law is a bit different. For example, it is possible to find *fatwa* accepting stunning since it is enough that the animal remains alive. The *fatwa* of the Mufti of Delhi in 1935 stated that it is permissible in ritual slaughtering to stun the animal as long as the animal does not die during the process. A similar view was exposed by the rector of the Al-Azhar University of Cairo in 1982. Furthermore, certain authorities maintain that Muslim law permits partaking of non-*halal* meat when *halal* meat is not available. But these opinions are, to a certain extent, controversial and there are those who rely on these decisions as applicable only to Muslims living in countries where there is no freedom of religion for them. . . .

Examining the Rights of Animals

One way to approach the problem of ritual slaughtering is to describe it as a conflict between two rights-holders, the religious individuals and the animals that are being slaughtered. If we pay careful attention to the language of the European Convention on rights, we ought to ask who, then, are these "others," whose rights and freedoms should be protected, and whether animals are included among these "others." This requires us to answer a basic question—is it possible at all to talk about "the rights of animals"? While it is not our intention to adopt a position about the question whether animals can be considered holders of rights at all, and a deep analysis of the philosophical issues involved is beyond the scope of this [viewpoint], it is necessary to advance some remarks on the topic, since it is not possible to see the guidelines of this debate without them. Yet, as we will show, we do not think that the determination that animals are rights-holders ultimately contributes to the solution of the problem of ritual slaughtering.

The debate over whether animals may be rights-holders is nothing new. We might begin with [philosopher and mathematician René] Descartes (1596–1650), who held the absolute view that animals had no rights whatsoever, and compared animals to machines (*automates*) without emotions. In his view, animals were incapable of suffering in the human sense, or, in any case, they had no consciousness of suffering, because they had nothing but reflexes. Descartes's position has been repeatedly assailed and today no one can seriously support it. A more balanced view, which takes into consideration the need to have compassion for animals, is expressed by [philosopher Immanuel] Kant, who recognizes that human beings have obligations toward animals, but no direct duties. In his view, animals have no self-awareness, and they are not regarded as an end in themselves but as means for the purposes of man.

In order to have rights, one must belong to "the same moral community" as those who have the authority and power to recognize rights.

During the nineteenth century, [philosopher Jeremy] Bentham took into consideration the suffering of animals but did not consider them holders of any rights. It is during the twentieth century that we see a more radical philosophical trend that is not content with the protection of animals (legal welfarism), but proposes to recognize a special rights-bearing status for animals. We note the views of two leaders of the intellectual movement supporting the cause of animal welfare, Peter Singer, who argues that utilitarianism requires taking into consideration the interests of animals, for "otherwise we fall into speciesism," and Tom Regan, the most prominent advocate of what we might call "the doctrine of rights." According to Regan, both human and nonhuman "subjects-of-a-life" have a basic moral right to respectful treatment, have inherent value, and thus enjoy an equal moral status. Accordingly, in his view, animals should be considered to have inherent rights. Still other scholars advocate against any exploitation of animals, though they derive their opposition to abuse of animals from different theoretical groundings.

On the other side, there are many philosophers who deny the concept of animal rights arguing that in order to have rights, one must belong to "the same moral community" as those who have the authority and power to recognize rights, and only those belonging to the same community are entitled to rights. In this view, since animals do not belong to the human moral community, they do not have rights. Still others, particularly those who hold the "choice theory of rights," believe that in order to have rights, an entity must have the capability of conscious choice between options for action and intentionally implement this choice. For them, an animal cannot choose; therefore, it has no rights.

Even if animals have no rights, that does not entail that we deny our obligations to them.

Inconsistencies in Approaches

There are many potential inconsistencies in the arguments of those who deny a special status to animals, as well as those who want to treat them as equal to human beings in terms of rights. For example, those who claim that one who has rights must be able to implement them cannot fully account for the fact that many human beings (babies, the mentally handicapped, etc.) cannot themselves make a legal appeal for their rights and yet most societies would hold that they still have rights. On the other hand, the recognition that some human beings not capable of conscious choice or of advocating for their rights still have rights does not require that a dog or a cat must always be treated under the law as a baby or as the mentally handicapped. The granting of rights to animals does

Kosher and Halal Food Practices

Knowledge of the kosher and halal dietary laws is important to the Jewish and Muslim populations who observe these laws and to food companies that wish to market to these populations and to interested consumers who do not observe these laws. The kosher dietary laws determine which foods are "fit or proper" for Jews and deal predominantly with 3 issues: allowed animals, the prohibition of blood, and the prohibition of mixing milk and meat. These laws are derived from the Torah and the oral law received by Moses on Mount Sinai (Talmud). Additional laws cover other areas such as grape products, cheese, baking, cooking, tithing, and foods that may not be eaten during the Jewish festival of Passover. Halal laws are derived from the Quran and the hadith, the traditions of the Prophet Muhammad. As with Kosher laws, there are specific allowed animals and a prohibition of the consumption of blood. Additionally, alcohol is prohibited.

J.M. Regenstein, M.M. Chaudry, and C.E. Regenstein,
"The Kosher and Halal Food Food Laws,"
Comprehensive Reviews in Food Science and Safety, *vol. 2, 2003.*

not entail the conclusion that they have the *same* rights as humans or suggest that their rights are more absolute than human rights. To make a facile equation between the two is tantamount to anthropomorphism an approach that surely should be avoided.

Notwithstanding the difficulty in assessing the moral rights of animals, and even assuming that they have no natural rights similar to human beings, there are cases where *the law* seems to recognize that animals have a certain sort of rights. In our view, however, this recognition in positive law cannot contribute very much to finding a clear framework for defining the status of animals. A positive law approach creates even more theoretical difficulties because to say that an animal has only those rights recognized by positive law leaves room to question whether there are animal rights not yet recognized by law. This approach leads to cumbersome discussions involving distinctions between "natural rights" and "positive rights," and will add nothing to the effective protection of the animals. Such debates simply divert us from finding the criteria we should use to determine whether certain animals are owed certain treatment by humans. The protection of animals should not become a debate about rights. As [ethicist Ronald] Dworkin explained, to talk about having rights is like claiming to have trump cards that enable rights advocates to control government or individual action toward them.

Even if we denied the recognition of animal rights, this does not mean that human beings would have an unlimited privilege to harm them or expose them to cruelty. Even if animals have no rights, that does not entail that we deny our *obligations* to them. For example, Peter Singer, a utilitarian, is reluctant to use the concept of "rights" to justify the obligations to defend and protect animals.

The Majority-Minority Rights Dynamic

Others have argued that the reason we protect animals is not because they have rights, but because we are protecting feelings of those humans who suffer from the suffering of animals, feelings which, of course, are shared by Jews and Muslims. However, governments must take the greatest care in moving from a focus on cruelty to animals to a focus on protecting the emotions of humans who suffer with them, not because it is improper to take into account the distress caused to humans when animals suffer, but because this interest does not always constitute a sufficient reason to impinge upon human freedom, particularly religious freedom, and specifically the religious freedom of minorities who have different views about the religious significance of animal slaughtering practices.

Even if there were a good case for comparing religious considerations to the emotional response of animal advocates, those advocates must produce very strong reasons indeed to explain why the feelings of someone who suffers when animals suffer should be juridically preferred over the right of someone to act according to his religious beliefs. From the point of view of the secular state, it might be possible to suggest that religious "feelings" are the same as cultural sentiments or national traditions, such as bullfighting in Spain. Even if it were possible to equate religious "feelings" to cultural or individual "feelings," however, in the ritual slaughtering case we are considering the majority's imposition of its religious beliefs and practices on a minority, rather than, as in Spain, the animal protection minority's advocacy to combat the practice against a democratic majority's decision to preserve the tradition. It is that majority-minority rights dynamic that is particularly problematical, as we will see. . . .

Prohibition Creates Discrimination

With regard to slaughtering, there is currently no way to justify a realistic abolitionist position since the majority of the public accepts the necessity of killing animals for food. But there is clearly a need to adopt a regulatory policy, so that slaughterhouses will provide more acceptable conditions for animals, notwithstanding that, or precisely because, they are going to be killed. The question is what values and orientations a regulatory framework should have, and what interests it should prefer. Animal protection regulations are bound to impinge on the interests of some sectors of the population, particularly those who will bear the economic effects of regulation. For example, regulations that specify how meat must be kept for sale in shops impose expense on shop owners, which they might consider an illegitimate restriction of their ownership rights and their freedom of occupation. Similarly, a prohibition against force-feeding geese that occurs to produce pate of a certain kind and quality hurts farmers who make a living from the practice. But these restrictions are different from the religious slaughter prohibition, because they apply to all shopkeepers and all farmers regardless of their religion or nationality, while the prohibition against religious slaughter applies only to certain groups with particular religious identities.

Using the ruse that one is attempting to protect an important value—the prevention of cruelty to animals—in order to attack a minority is not such a difficult thing to do and even if lawmakers are well intentioned, the prohibition of ritual slaughtering will still fall under a certain degree of suspicion as reflective of anti-Jewish or anti-Muslim sentiment, so we should be cautious before accepting arguments at face value or conceding them too quickly.

Animal protection regulations are bound to impinge on the interests of some sectors of the population.

Any regulatory framework that prohibits ritual slaughtering is likely to be infected with elements of religious discrimination since it is easy for those who would use the cloak of animal protection for other ends, such as attacking those whose religious beliefs differ from their own. One can see such examples in other contexts, such as when a tenant's keeping pets is used as an excuse for evicting him because the landlord does not like him, or when a local population objects to a dam that interferes with the status quo in their community using the excuse that they are protecting fish that are in danger of extinction.

South Africa's Ritual Slaughters Do Not Supersede the Rights of Animals

Kevin Behrens

Kevin Behrens is a doctoral student in the Department of Philosophy at the University of Johannesburg in South Africa. In the following viewpoint, he argues that the ritual slaughter of animals is not morally defensible. He acknowledges the custom of killing animals for cultural reasons, such as the cleansing ceremony following a prison release, but finds these acts inhumane and unnecessary.

As you read, consider the following questions:

1. What does the author mean by "*prima facie* wrong"?
2. What are some examples Behrens identifies as "soft" human interests?
3. How could the ritual slaughter of animals be made morally justifiable, according to the author?

The ritual slaughter of a bull as a traditional cleansing ceremony for the family of [South African politician] Tony Yengeni after his release from prison occasioned much public and media debate. Animal rights and anticruelty proponents raised concerns about how the animal was killed, claiming

Kevin Behrens, "Tony Yengeni's Ritual Slaughter: Animal Anti-Cruelty vs. Culture," *South African Journal of Philosophy*, vol. 28, no. 3, 2009, pp. 271–272, 283–285, 288.

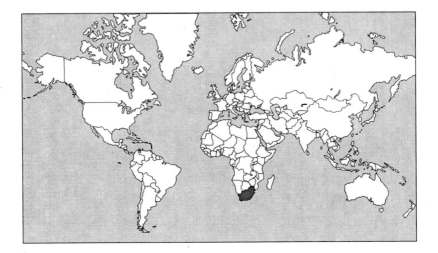

that the action constituted cruelty, and transgressed anticruelty laws. In response, others claimed that such practices are a
fundamental part of the culture of some groups in South Africa, essential to their sense of identity, and as such should not
be interfered with.

Questions of Morality

This incident highlights two contentious trends in current
normative ethical debate. On the one hand, there have been
growing calls for more ethical treatment of animals, for some
animals, at least, to be accorded some value as objects of
moral consideration, and even for animals to be understood
as possessing rights. On the other hand, in an increasingly
multicultural context, many call for stronger measures to ensure the protection of minority or disadvantaged cultures
against the encroachment of more dominant cultures. Appeals
are made for special protective measures and legislation, and
again, some even claim the existence of cultural rights. On a
popular level, frequent appeals are made to culture as providing moral justification for particular practices.

The extent of the public debate over the Yengeni ritual
slaughter indicates that these areas of ethical contention are

pertinent in the South African context. What makes this incident particularly interesting is that it pits claims of moral concern for animals against claims for the moral defence of a traditional practice on (human) cultural grounds. Since both kinds of claim are contentious, calculating the relative moral weight of the claims against each other is no easy task. In this [viewpoint] I shall attempt to do just that.

Claims based on the moral value of cultural identification or participation are, at best, relatively weak moral claims.

The question I address is the following: 'Are acts of the ritual slaughter of animals, of the kind recently engaged in by the Yengeni family, morally justifiable?' . . .

The central thesis I wish to defend is that ritual animal sacrifice of this kind is a *prima facie* wrong, since, it causes animals, unnecessary suffering. By '*prima facie* wrong' I mean the kind of act which is normally wrong but the wrongness of which could, in certain circumstances, possibly be outweighed by other moral considerations which would render the act justified. My position is that in rituals of this kind, claims based on the moral value of cultural identification or participation are, at best, relatively weak moral claims, which are *not* able to outweigh the *prima facie* wrong of causing animals harm.

Human Interests Versus Animal Welfare

Consider a case where a relatively trivial human interest conflicts with the interests of animals not to be hurt or tortured. An example of this might be the 'sport' of dogfighting. I take it that the primary human interest in this activity is recreational. The participants claim that they derive enjoyment from watching this sport, and perhaps from the gambling that often accompanies it. Is this human recreational interest sufficiently morally significant to outweigh the harm done to the dogs involved? These animals are deliberately bred to encourage violent traits, and are then forced to fight other dogs, often leading to vicious, violent encounters, and to obvious pain, suffering and even death for the dogs involved. It would be difficult for any philosopher to defend such a practice morally on the grounds that human interests always trump those of animals. On such grounds it could be argued that no amount of animal suffering can outweigh even a small and relatively unimportant human interest. For example, massive cruelty to animals for the sake of human vanity would be 'legitimised' on such a position. Our moral intuitions seem to balk at this conception, and these intuitions are probably at the root of the banning of dogfighting as a 'sport' in many parts of the world.

However, even if we grant that human interests are not always more weighty than those of animals, surely a case can be made that they sometimes are. Perhaps there are times when animals may need to be harmed for the sake of more weighty human interests. This is not to say that human interests always outweigh those of animals, but that some human interests can possibly carry more moral weight. In such cases, pain caused to animals could be understood to be necessary, even if regrettable.

Perhaps there are times when animals may need to be harmed for the sake of more weighty human interests.

Human Health and Lives Versus Animal Welfare

Some kinds of vivisection, particularly for the testing of medicines, are often justified on these sorts of grounds. Many would regard suffering caused to animals for this purpose as lamentable, but justified. Since I have taken the position that we may owe more to humans morally than to animals, this could seem plausible. Whilst I do not wish to launch a defence of animal experimentation here, in cases where the health and, indeed, lives of large numbers of people could be preserved as a result of medical trials involving animal subjects, a case could be made that some animal suffering for this end might be morally justifiable. To my mind, this would require the further condition that there would be no other means to perform this testing that would be as effective or cause less harm. The important point, though, is that what is at stake here is the health and lives of people. These sorts of human interests are clearly morally much more weighty than interest in, say, recreation. They might be construed to provide good enough reasons for justifying some animal suffering on behalf of people.

If such nontrivial human interests can sometimes outweigh the *prima facie* wrong of harming animals deliberately, can a similar case not be made that the continued participation of cultures in the practice of ritual slaughter of the type under discussion provides social goods of significant enough moral importance to justify the harm caused to animals in these rituals? To answer this I need to consider again the moral values inherent in cultural identification I identified in the previous section. It might be argued that if people were to negatively judge the practices of other cultures (even without advocating their social restriction) they could cause harm to the members of those cultures. Taking a negative stance towards a cultural practice could deny members of a culture some of the social goods which might be obtained through their identification with and participation in their culture, and their expression of authenticity. If someone says that what one does in one's culture is wrong, she could challenge a fundamental part of one's perceived identity, and possibly also one's self-esteem, dignity, etc. I have already stated that I have sympathy with the claim of previously disparaged cultures that they have a morally significant claim that their interests in identification and the recovery of their group self-esteem be acknowledged. But are the social goods or interests that could be denied to such cultures by morally questioning an aspect of their cultural practice significant enough to outweigh the interests of animals not to be harmed?

The dignity and esteem of a cultural group is not denied by questioning the morality of a specific traditional practice.

'Soft' Human Interests

I return to the thought experiment I considered a little earlier. Imagine again a situation in which a person with deep psychological problems could be greatly assisted by a therapeutic intervention involving her physically assaulting, in this case, not another human being, but say, a household pet. Would the possible psychological healing that might result outweigh the *prima facie* wrong of harming an animal? Intuitively, I think most people would find this difficult to accept. At the very least we would wonder whether similar therapeutic results could not be achieved using other less cruel methods, such as employing perhaps a stuffed toy animal, to represent a pet.

'Soft' human interests such as psychological welfare, esteem, authenticity, etc., do not as easily pass the muster of being obviously more moral weighty than animal interests in not being harmed, in quite the same way as more basic human interests in life, health and bodily integrity seem to do. That notwithstanding, this thought experiment deals with the psychological well-being of an individual human being. A further objection to my position could be that with cultural interests or social goods, there is a collective benefit to be taken into account, too. For people who have suffered generations of repression and cultural denigration, is the free practice of their culture now not a vitally important component of redis-

Modern Freedoms of Religion and Culture

On Sunday, January 20, 2007, Tony Yengeni, former Chief Whip of South Africa's governing party, the African National Congress (ANC), celebrated his early release from a four-year prison sentence by slaughtering a bull at his father's house in the Cape Town township of Gugulethu. This time-honored African ritual was performed in order to appease the Yengeni family ancestors. Animal rights activists, however, decried the sacrifice as an act of unnecessary cruelty to the bull, and a public outcry ensued. Leading figures in government circles ... entered the fray, calling for a proper understanding of African cultural practices. Jody Kollapen, the chair of the [South African] Human Rights Commission, said: "the slaughter of animals by cultures in South Africa was an issue that needed to be dealt with in context. Cultural liberty is an important right...."

That the sacrifice was defended on the ground of African culture was to be expected. More surprising was the way in which everyone involved in the affair ignored what could have been regarded as an event of religious significance. Admittedly, it is far from easy to separate the concepts of religion and culture ... in certain societies.... Today in South Africa, however, it is clearly necessary to make such a distinction for human rights litigation, partly because the Constitution specifies religion and culture as two separate rights and partly because it seems that those working under the influence of modern human rights seem to take religion more seriously than culture.

Jewel Amoah and Tom Bennett,
"The Freedoms of Religion and Culture Under
the South African Constitution: Do Traditional
African Religions Enjoy Equal Treatment?"
Journal of Law & Religion, *vol. 24, no. 1, 2008–2009.*

covering their worth and meaning as a whole group? The sense of recovery of dignity of such peoples can hardly be thought of as a trivial human interest. Indeed, it might be argued that such concerns could be weighty enough to argue that the pain caused to animals in ritual slaughter might be considered necessary.

My first line of defence against this position is that taking a moral position against a single cultural practice, and more specifically only to one aspect of this practice (namely the method of slaughter used in rituals) cannot be construed as significantly denying members of a culture the possibility of increased dignity and group esteem to be gained from cultural participation. Cultures are characterised by many different values, norms, practices, rites, and behaviours. To acknowledge and respect the interests of others derived from their cultural identification does not necessarily require that every one of the elements that contribute to that culture must necessarily be regarded as outside of the scope of moral judgment or criticism. One can plausibly, broadly respect the interests based in cultural identification of many indigenous South Africans, without granting that cultural practices involving animal suffering are morally justified. The dignity and esteem of a cultural group is not denied by questioning the morality of a specific traditional practice, and nor would such questioning necessarily significantly deprive them of the moral values derived from cultural identification. . . .

Inhumane Ritual Slaughter Is Morally Unjustifiable

Since animal suffering is very likely to occur in ritual slaughters of the kind performed by the Yengeni family, it does not seem to me that this kind of act can be morally justified on the grounds that it is a traditional or religiously required practice, central to the culture of the people involved. At best, culture provides weak grounds for defending practices morally. The interests of sentient beings not to be hurt must carry more moral weight than the interests of humans in the social goods or moral values derived from cultural identification and participation. Furthermore, taking moral exception to a particular cultural practice and especially merely to one aspect of the practice cannot be construed as significantly denying those who perform this practice of the social goods or values derived from their cultural participation.

The moral value or social goods derived from cultural practice are not significant enough to outweigh the *prima facie* wrong of harming animals in ritual sacrifices. On these grounds I conclude that acts of the ritual slaughter of animals, of the kind recently engaged in by the Yengeni family are not morally justifiable, although they could be, if the method of slaughter were modified to include pre-stunning.

At best, culture provides weak grounds for defending practices morally.

I have, thus far, excluded issues of the role of the law in situations such as this. In my concluding remarks, however, I wish to consider this angle. I am not at all convinced that the best way to deal with this moral conflict is by means of legislation. It is not always necessary to manage moral conflicts by means of legal proscription. Perhaps the best way forward is for those on both sides of this moral debate to enter into discussion with one another. Perhaps a way can be found to accommodate the interests of cultures to experience the benefits of cultural identification and authenticity, as well as those of healing and restoration, without needing to cause animals unnecessary suffering. Perhaps those who seek some kind of relief from their own painful experiences by means of ritual practices could find even more meaningful relief by modifying their cultural practices in a way which demonstrates their empathy with the suffering of other sentient beings.

Jews Should Become Vegetarians to Respect Animal Rights

Daniel Brook

In the following viewpoint Daniel Brook, instructor of sociology at San José State University, argues that the Jewish faith supports and encourages followers to be vegetarians. Not only is not eating meat healthier, but abstaining from animal products also respects animal rights and helps to conserve natural resources. In addition, Brook asserts that the meat industry contributes to the world's hunger and global violence.

As you read, consider the following questions:

1. What fraction of US crops are fed to animals in the meat industry, according to Brook?
2. What fraction of diseases in the United States does Brook say are diet related?
3. How does the author describe vegetarianism as eco-kashrut?

Judaism has to be a daily spiritual and social practice, not simply a ritualized one, if it is to be meaningful to Jews and relevant to others. Beyond being spiritual, we are called upon to uplift ourselves and to make the world a better place for ourselves, our families, our communities, and others.

In *Why Be Jewish?* Rabbi David J. Wolpe writes that "Judaism emphasizes good deeds because nothing else can replace them. To love justice and decency, to hate cruelty and to thirst for righteousness—that is the essence of the human task." The human task, therefore, is to be a *mensch*: a good, kind, and compassionate person.

One of the ways to follow our rich tradition while putting Judaism's highest ideals into daily practice is to choose vegetarianism. In the words of Rabbi Fred Scherlinder Dobb, "I see vegetarianism as a *mitzvah*"—a sacred duty and good deed.

The human task ... is to be a mensch: *a good, kind, and compassionate person.*

[Medieval Jewish philosopher] [Moses] Maimonides postulated thirteen principles of the Jewish faith, while Rabbi Moses Cordovero wrote about "The Thirteen Divine Attributes." Here are [several] categorical imperatives suggesting why Jews should seriously consider vegetarianism and then move in that direction:

Righteousness and Charity. Even though it is often difficult, we do all have the power to break bad habits and soul search for better ways of living. Becoming vegetarian sets a lifelong course of righteousness. Righteous people regard—and guard—the lives of animals. According to [scientist and philosopher] Albert Einstein, if people aspire toward a righteous life, their "first act of abstinence is from injury to animals." A *tzadik*, or righteous person, is held in the highest regard because of righteous actions. . . .

Judaism stresses the importantce of *tzedakah*, that we be kind, assist the poor and weak, and share our food with the hungry. Yet about three-fourths of major U.S. crops such as corn, wheat, soybeans, oats, and alfalfa are fed to the billions of animals destined to be slaughtered for meat, while millions of people worldwide die from hunger and its cruel effects each year. This is an avoidable *shanda* (shame) on the world. . . .

Thousands of gallons of fresh water are wasted merely to produce a single pound of beef.

Consideration for Our Environment

Tikkun Olam. While Judaism teaches that we are to be *shomrei adamah*, partners in *tikkun olam*—recreating, preserving, and healing the world—mass production of meat contributes substantially to greenhouse gas emission and global warming (what Rabbi Arthur Waskow calls "global scorching," and what the United Nations says is "the most serious challenge facing the human race"). Meat production also contributes to air and water pollution; overuse of chemicals and fossil fuels; the deforestation and destruction of tropical rain forests, coral reefs, mangroves, and other habitats; soil erosion; desertification; species extinction; loss of biodiversity; and various other forms of global environmental degradation. Among other things, we need to re-establish and reinvigorate the earth's *mayim chayim*—its living waters. . . .

Conservation of Resources. Judaism teaches *bal tashchit* (concern for the environment), that we should not waste or unnecessarily destroy anything of value (in other words, engage in conservation), and that we should not use more than what is necessary to accomplish a purpose (in other words, prioritize efficiency). Yet, in contrast to these Jewish values, meat production requires the very wasteful use of land, top soil, water, fossil fuels and other forms of energy, labor, grain, and other vital resources, in addition to various toxic chemicals, antibiotics, and hormones. For example, it can require approximately seventy-eight calories of nonrenewable fossil fuel for each calorie of protein obtained from factory-farmed beef, but only two calories of fossil fuel to produce a calorie of protein from soybeans. Thousands of gallons of fresh water are wasted merely to produce a single pound of beef. . . .

Responsibility for Human Health

Health and Safety. Health and the protection of life are repeatedly emphasized, and even prioritized, in Jewish teachings. While Judaism teaches that we should be very careful about *sh'mirat haguf* (preserving our bodies and health), and *pekuach nefesh* (protecting our lives at almost any cost), numerous scientific studies have linked animal-based diets directly to heart disease and heart attacks (the number one cause of death in the United States), various forms of cancer (the number two cause of death), stroke (the number three cause of death), high blood pressure, obesity, diabetes, osteoporosis, asthma, atherosclerosis, aneurysms, rheumatoid arthritis, impotence, endometriosis, gallstones, gout, Alzheimer's [disease], and other ailments. About two-thirds of diseases in the United States are diet related—and vegetarians are much less afflicted. Note that even meat-eating doctors almost always recommend eating less meat, not more, while advocating the consumption of more fresh fruit, vegetables, beans, and whole grains for better health.

The meat industry is unhealthy and unsafe.

Further, since more than half of all antibiotics in the United States are given to livestock (plus immense amounts of chemicals, steroids, hormones, and other drugs), resistant bacteria are increasing at an alarming rate, creating untreatable superbugs, like MRSA, that kill tens of thousands of people per year in the United States alone. And don't forget mad cow disease, bird flu, foot and mouth disease, *E. coli*, *Salmonella*, and food poisoning. "If there were no poultry industry," concludes Neal Barnard, M.D., "there would be no epidemics of bird flu." And if there were no cow industry, there would be no *E. coli* outbreaks.

Jewish Scholars Believe God Intended Man to Be Vegetarian

Scholars of Judaism agree that God's intention was for man to be vegetarian. "God did not permit Adam and his wife to kill a creature and to eat its flesh," said Rashi, a highly respected, 12th-century Jewish rabbi who wrote the first comprehensive commentaries on the Talmud and Tanakh. Ronald Isaacs states in *Animals in Jewish Thought and Tradition* that all Talmudic rabbis include that "the permission to eat meat [was granted to human kind] as a compromise, a divine concession to human weakness and human need." Rabbi Elijah Judah Schochet, in *Animal Life in Jewish Tradition*, notes that "scripture does not command the Israelite to eat meat, but permits this diet as a concession to lust."

Jane Srivastava,
"Vegetarianism and Meat-Eating in 8 Religions,"
Hinduism Today, *April–June 2007.*

Packaged meat has been discovered to be injected with carbon monoxide to keep it looking red, even when it's rancid. Fish often contain mercury, arsenic, lead, cadmium and toxic POPs [persistent organic pollutants], including PCBs, DDT, and dioxin, which can't be removed from the fish and which bioaccumulate in consumers' bodies.

The meat industry is unhealthy and unsafe. A vegetarian diet (one that does not include *any* animals) or a vegan diet (a vegetarian diet that does not include any animal products at all, including meat, dairy, and eggs) can help prevent, and sometimes reverse, many of these health- and life-threatening conditions. . . .

Jewish Spirituality

Knowledge and Spirituality. Judaism often emphasizes the interplay between thinking and doing, highlighting the vital role of *kavanah* (spiritual intention and concentration) as a precondition for action. That is a motivation behind the blessings, of which there is none specifically for meat—unlike for grains, fruits, and vegetables. According to Jewish tradition, meat-eating was permitted, with elaborate restrictions, after the Flood of Noah as a temporary concession to the human weakness of those with a "lust for meat." It is also part of our teaching, from Hillel's disagreement with Shamai over the lighting of the Chanukah menorah recounted in the Talmud, that *ma'alin bakodesh v'ayn moridim*: in sacred matters we must increase in holiness rather than decrease. We can increase our holiness by making our consumption more holy.

For those who erroneously think it might be a mitzvah to eat meat during holy days, it is a *mitzvah haba'ah al y'dei aveirah*, a mitzvah that derives from a sin; it is the fruit of a poisonous tree, and therefore no mitzvah at all. Citing Jewish law, Rabbi Adam Frank says, "The end user of a product knowingly derived by cruel means is a participant in the cruelty." Rabbi Frank adds: "Modern, secular thinking allows for sentient creatures to be treated like inanimate objects, but Jewish tradition does not. ... My decision to abstain from the consumption of animal products is an expression of my adherence to Jewish law, and it expresses my disapproval and disdain for the cruel practices of the industry." ...

We can increase our holiness by making our consumption more holy.

Divinity. The scholar and mystic Rabbi Moses Cordovero (1522–1570 CE) wrote a manual on ethics titled "The Thirteen Divine Attributes." He included meditation exercises involving the visualization of one's body as the Tree of Life, while focusing on a particular aspect of the Tree, or body. The meat industry is responsible for a tremendous amount of deforestation, cutting down, burning, and clearing millions of trees each day, destroying about an acre of Amazon rain forest every second, thereby also displacing or killing the people, animals, and plants living there.

The meat industry is making mincemeat out of the rain forests, which are often referred to as "the lungs of the planet," essentially converting this amazing life-sustaining resource into carbon dioxide and cholesterol, significantly contributing to both planetary and personal ill health. In a miracle of continuing co-evolutionary development, as Rabbi Arthur Waskow discusses, we breathe in the oxygen that trees breathe out, while we breathe out the carbon dioxide that trees breathe in. We need each other and breathe each other into continued existence, yet the production and consumption of meat is killing the trees of life, ignoring both science and Torah. . . .

Promoting Global Harmony

Peace and Justice. Judaism repeatedly stresses that we must always seek and pursue *shalom v'tzedek* (peace and justice) and that moral degradation and violence result from unjust conditions. Animal-centered diets waste valuable resources and desensitize us to violence. Such diets help to perpetuate the widespread poverty, hunger, environmental destruction, and despair that lead to mass suffering, social insecurity, ethnic hostilities, violence, genocide, and war. . . .

Vegetarianism creates conditions that are more fair and just, more efficient and sustainable, and more healthy, thereby potentially allowing more people to be fed, rather than using land, grain, water, labor, energy, and other resources to inefficiently and immorally produce food to be fed to animals that are later killed and fed to a smaller number of more affluent people.

Keeping Kosher. The practice of *kashrut*, or keeping kosher, is the specific way of applying Jewish teachings and Jewish values to our consumption of food. Besides being life sustaining, satisfying, and often joyous, eating is a holy act. And as Rabbi Pinchas Peli writes in *Torah Today*, "The laws of kashrut come to teach us that a Jew's first preference should be a vegetarian meal." Further, Rabbi Robert Gordis states, "Vegetarianism offers an ideal mode for preserving the religious and ethical values which kashrut was designed to concretize in human life." Indeed, as Rabbi Daniel Jezer says, "A higher form of being kosher is vegetarianism."

Animal-centered diets waste valuable resources and desensitize us to violence.

Vegetarianism, as a form of eco-kashrut, is an easy and effective way to keep kosher, to be more sustainable, to be more healthy, and to be more holy. In this sense, all meat is *treyf*, unkosher and unfit for human consumption. Rabbi Jonathan Sacks, chief rabbi of the United Hebrew Congregations of the Commonwealth, commented that "I'm a vegetarian and I stay *milchik* all the time." Similarly, Rabbi Shear-Yashuv Cohen, Ashkenazi Chief Rabbi of Haifa, Israel, said, "If you don't eat meat, you are certainly kosher, and I believe that is what we should tell our fellow rabbis."

Fighting Fascism. Historically, and unfortunately still presently, Jews have been common targets of authoritarian, fascist, and genocidal policies and actions, whatever their names and places. Jewish ethics, Jewish values, and even the method of the Talmud itself, respects and protects minority opinions and minority groups. "Just as the Nazis dehumanized the Jews in their propaganda and in the atrocities they committed," writes Jay Levine, M.D., "the apologists for meat consumption and the exploitation of animals have stereotyped and degraded the animal kingdom for their own purposes, declaring animals to be devoid of cognitive functioning and even of pain."

It is important to note that "the Nazis explicitly structured their industrial destruction of the Jews [and other peoples] on the model of animal slaughter," according to Rabbi Hillel Norry. "This is not to compare the suffering of animals and humans, but shows that the way we treat animals is similar to the way the Nazis treated us." . . .

What we do to animals and the environment, therefore, we are ultimately doing to ourselves and our community.

The Global Community

Vegetarianism helps us to preserve and protect our health, environment, culture, community, society, and spirit *l'dor vador*, from generation to generation. Ecclesiastes, which is attributed to King Solomon, says: "The fate of men and the fate of animals, they have one and the same fate. As one dies, so does the other, and they all have the same spirit." What we do to animals and the environment, therefore, we are ultimately doing to ourselves and our communities. We are fouling our own nest.

Christians Should Treat Animals Humanely

Michael Morris

Michael Morris teaches zoology at the New Zealand Centre for Human-Animal Studies at the University of Canterbury. In the following viewpoint, he argues that Christian teaching encourages respect of animals, including those used in the food chain. Using evidence from the Bible, Morris supports his assertions that humans should treat animals humanely as God's creatures. Current farming practices do the opposite; therefore, Morris urges Christian churches to make their events free of meat or at least offer more nonanimal-based options.

As you read, consider the following questions:

1. According to the viewpoint, around how many animals are raised and slaughtered each year in the United States?

2. What percentage of hens suffer from broken bones when being handled for slaughter, as Morris reports?

3. For what animal-based items does the author make exception to be served at Christian church events?

Michael Morris, "How Should Christians Treat Animals?" *Stimulus, THE NEW ZEALAND JOURNAL OF CHRISTIAN THOUGHT AND PRACTICE,* vol. 15, no. 4, November 2007, pp. 59–63. Copyright © 2007 by *Stimulus, THE NEW ZEALAND JOURNAL OF CHRISTIAN THOUGHT AND PRACTICE.* Reproduced by permission.

Rather than using Christian or secular arguments as a way of expanding our view of stewardship or the "rights" of animals, I have therefore chosen to accept two traditional evangelical assumptions claiming a unique place of human beings in creation, namely:

- That the difference in kind between humans and animals is related to our ability to show spiritual, as well as natural, awareness and to form a spiritual relationship with God.

- That this difference is such that God will allow us to place our own interests above those of nonhuman animals.

I will argue that even if we accept the above assumptions, it does not follow logically that animals have only the same inherent value as the rest of creation, or that the only interest we need to take into account is that the animal does not suffer.

It does not follow logically that animals have only the same inherent value as the rest of creation.

The Moral Status of Animals

It is generally believed that animals are distinct from the rest of nonhuman creation, in that they are capable of feeling pain. It is their capacity for feeling pain that has historically formed the basis for the ethical imperative that they must not be made to suffer. In recent times, it has become apparent that animals can feel pleasure as well as pain. The basis of inferring these feelings is the argument from analogy. Animals behave in similar ways to a human under a circumstance in which we would infer pain or pleasure in the human subject. Animals also have a nervous system and physiological responses to painful or pleasurable stimuli that are very similar to humans. If we are willing to infer consciousness in humans other than ourselves, then it is logically inconsistent not to conclude that animals have the same modes of awareness.

There are also theological grounds for accepting that animal life contains an excess of pleasure over pain. God is good, and the apostle Paul tells us that present sufferings are "not worth comparing with the glory that will be revealed in us." If God made animals with the capability of feeling pain, then it should be apparent that a loving God would compensate with a capacity for pleasure in greater abundance. There is also biblical evidence that God cares for the lives of animals, often grouping animals together with humans, and that before sin entered the world God did not build in a dependence or desire for animal flesh in either human or nonhuman animals.

If we can accept that animals can feel pleasure then it is not necessary to infer a spiritual dimension to their lives to know that God has presented them with one extra gift common to God and to humans but not to non-sentient beings. Ending of the life of an animal cuts short this gift of God, and therefore harms it in a real way. . . .

There is . . . biblical evidence that God cares for the lives of animals.

The Christian tradition bases the moral status of humans on their being made in the image of God and therefore having a special relationship with the Creator, not on awareness alone. This accounts for the special protection many Christians give to the unborn, the severely mentally ill, and the comatose, whose awareness may be minimal or nonexistent. In the case of humans, the belief in the intrinsic value of human life and its spiritual dimension may take precedence even over the desires of its owners, which is why some Christians take a strong view on euthanasia and condemn suicide.

Nevertheless, it is the presence of awareness in humans which is seen to provide evidence for the special relationship our species enjoys with God. [Thirteenth-century philosopher and theologian] Thomas Aquinas for example claims rationality for humans alone, and dismisses concern for animals on the basis that they are "irrational." Such a belief has permeated Western culture to the extent that it is only in the last couple of centuries that our relationship to animals as rational beings is taken seriously. It is now becoming apparent in both the secular and Christian tradition that animals are far from "brute beasts that have no understanding." If human awareness is seen as proof of our special relationship with God, it is inconsistent not to concede that higher animals such as the ones we eat every day also deserve special consideration.

The Church [must take] a stand on forms of ritualised animal abuse common to modern society.

If animals lack a spiritual dimension, such consideration need not extend to preserving the life of an animal against its own interest. This means that involuntary euthanasia is an appropriate and loving response to an animal suffering from severe pain from which it cannot recover. A Christian who worships a sentient, self-aware God with beliefs, desires and emotions does however need to take into consideration seriously the individual interests of animals who share these features. This necessitates the Church taking a stand on forms of ritualised animal abuse common to modern society that clearly act against the interests of animals. The most pervasive of these is the use of their flesh, milk and eggs for food. Since this is also behaviour that is most easily modified at an individual or church level, I have described the practices of intensive ("factory") farming below in more detail.

Factory Farming Breeds Suffering

A recent estimate is that 10 billion land animals—almost twice the human population—are raised and slaughtered each year in the United States alone. No other usage of animals compares in terms of its wide acceptance. Christians often excuse the practice on the basis of its widespread use in the Bible. For example, God specifically gave permission for Noah and his descendants to eat animals; there are the numerous accounts of sacrifice in the Old Testament; Jesus himself saw no problem in killing the fatted calf for the return of the prodigal son, and God gave permission for Peter to "kill and eat" a number of different clean and unclean beasts. . . .

Even if we restrict our duties to animals to the avoidance of suffering, it is apparent that the degree of suffering experienced by animals in the modern factory farm is incomparably greater than that suffered in the free-range farming practised in biblical times.

Pigs in Western societies for example are routinely kept in narrow stalls for their entire lives, where they are unable to perform any of their normal functions or even to turn around. This narrow confinement leads not only to debilitating physical illnesses caused through lack of exercise and cramped conditions, but also to severe psychological trauma leading to stereotyped behaviour indicative of insanity.

Layer hens are similarly confined, several to a cage, in an area that provides each hen with less space than an A4 sheet of paper [about 8.5 by 11 inches]. This severe confinement leads to a number of physical illnesses and deformities, including weakening and fracturing of bones. When layer hens are handled prior to slaughter, the general weakening of their bones means that up to 30% of hens suffer from broken bones when being handled before slaughter. To prevent cannibalism and feather pecking, hens have their beaks trimmed when they are a day old, an operation which results in extreme acute and long-term pain. But the worst form of deprivation must be the inability for hens to display any of the natural behaviour they enjoy, including dust bathing, foraging, nesting, or even flapping their wings. . . .

Animal products should be totally avoided at church events.

Making Lifestyle Changes

Animals may not be created as images of God in such a clear manner as humans, but nevertheless do possess many of the attributes of their Creator. It is therefore inconsistent not to provide them with at least some of the rights accorded to *Homo sapiens* in the Christian tradition. If taken seriously, this requires a radical rethink about the way we treat animals, and will necessitate some lifestyle changes among Christians. . . .

If the lives of animals as individuals are to mean anything, then animal products should be totally avoided at church events, with the possible exception of free-range eggs, shell fish, humanely killed fish and crustaceans, and dairy products sourced from cruelty-free suppliers. However, this would probably alienate many members of the congregation, and if adopted in a wholesale fashion may do more harm than good. A more gradual change could therefore be in order. It should be possible for example to avoid the products derived from the worst expresses of factory farming (pig meat, chicken and battery "caged" eggs), and to ensure that vegetarian and vegan options are available for those with moral objections to eating animal products. It has also been my experience that if nutritious and appealing vegetarian and vegan options are presented at functions, then even hard-core carnivores are inclined to take them in preference to their usual fare, and even exclaim that they did not realise vegan food tasted so good. Providing a variety of food options could therefore be more conducive to opening hearts and minds than a blanket prohibition.

Unfortunately, the Church has made little progress in making these concessions to its vegetarian and vegan members. An article in a popular Christian magazine lamented the fact that churches in the United States not only are unwilling to stop serving flesh at church events, but that they show more reluctance than the general society to accommodate those who have chosen an alternative diet. Vegetarian and vegan options are common at secular potluck events, but not at their Christian counterparts. I can confirm that the same attitude prevails in New Zealand churches. One churchgoer objected to this criticism pointing out that salads are always available at church barbecues. But this proves my point. A salad is no more a complete meal for a vegan than it is for an omnivore, and treating them as if they have fewer nutritional requirements than the general population shows a lack of understanding, and indeed could be construed as discriminatory. Neglect, hostility or indifference towards those with a different view to the mainstream is certainly not appropriate, given the general biblical exhortation to accommodate to those whose expression of faith is different from our own.

Concern for animals is quite compatible with traditional evangelical assumptions of the special place of humans.

If churches took the lead in abstaining from most animal products, this would send a strong message to the rest of society and in itself would achieve a great deal for animals. The realisation that animals should form part of our moral concern also has ramifications in other areas that have not been discussed, such as vivisection and genetic modification of animals. In some ways, the present lack of concern for animals is an historical anomaly among the Christian community. In the past, Christians have played a major part in the animal liberation movement and theological arguments for a better treatment of animals largely preceded scientific ones.

Returning to Traditional Christian Compassion

One reason for the present lack of concern may be that the animal liberation movement has largely been co-opted by Darwinian materialists [with a focus on evolution], and with it has come hostility towards the Christian view of humans having a special place in the universe. An indifference to animals may be a defensive reaction to what Christians perceive as a threat from the secular side.

However, as I have tried to show, concern for animals is quite compatible with traditional evangelical assumptions of the special place of humans. As another Christian commentator has said, there is no danger that showing compassion to animals will knock humanity from its pedestal. Christians have worked together with those holding different beliefs when campaigning for better treatment of slaves, workers, prisoners and other marginalised members of society. There is no reason why Christians and non-Christians cannot similarly put their other differences to one side, while working together to make the world a better place for nonhuman animals.

Periodical and Internet Sources Bibliography

The following articles have been selected to supplement the diverse views presented in this chapter.

Richard Ballard	"'Slaughter in the Suburbs': Livestock Slaughter and Race in Post-Apartheid Cities," *Ethnic and Racial Studies*, vol. 33, no. 6, June 2010.
Marc Bekoff	"Increasing Our Compassion Footprint: The Animals' Manifesto," *Zygon: Journal of Religion & Science*, vol. 43, no. 4, December 2008.
Andy Coghlan	"Animals Feel the Pain of Religious Slaughter," *New Scientist*, October 2009.
Rebecca Evans	"Bullfighting Banned in Catalonia," *Daily Mirror* (UK), July 29, 2010.
Jeff Goodell	"The Poisoning," *Rolling Stone*, July 21, 2010.
Lorne Jackson	"Ask Not for Whom the Beer Belly Tolls," *Sunday Mercury* (Birmingham, England), August 1, 2010.
Richard Kool	"'What Goes Around Comes Around': Prohibitions to Cruelty Against Animals in Judaism," *Worldviews: Global Religions, Culture, and Ecology*, vol. 14, no. 1, 2010.
Valerie K. Sims, Matthew G. Chin, and Ryan E. Yordon	"Don't Be Cruel: Assessing Beliefs About Punishments for Crimes Against Animals," *Anthrozoos*, vol. 20, no. 3, September 2007.
Peter Singer	"Religion's Regressive Hold on Animal Rights Issues," guardian.co.uk, June 8, 2010.
Ian W. Thomson	"Ban Barbaric Boxing as Well as Bull-Fighting," *Herald* (Glasgow, UK), August 3, 2010.
David Von Drehle	"Can Attack Dogs Be Rehabilitated," *Time*, December 7, 2009.

CHAPTER 2

Animal Welfare and Global Biomedical Research

Animal Experimentation Is Necessary for the Well-Being of Humans

Stanley N. Gershoff

In the following viewpoint, Stanley N. Gershoff, Dean Emeritus of the Gerald J. and Dorothy R. Friedman School of Nutrition Science and Policy at Tufts University, argues that using animals in experiments is necessary for the health of human beings. Using many historical examples, Gershoff states that animals have played an important role in finding the cure of many lethal diseases, including diseases afflicting other animals. Although he does not believe that animals have rights, he does believe that care should be taken when using them in experiments.

As you read, consider the following questions:

1. How does the viewpoint identify beriberi?
2. What is "running fits," according to Gershoff?
3. Why does Gershoff say the United States government recently seized 140 millions pounds of beef?

The debate about animal experimentation is frequently outrageous, with both sides making statements that are clearly misleading. Much more disturbing, however, are the illegal terrorist attacks by groups opposed to animal experi-

Stanley N. Gershoff, "Animal Experimentation—A Personal View," *Nutrition Reviews*, vol. 67, no. 2, February 2009, pp. 95–99. Copyright © 2009 by *Nutrition Reviews*. Reproduced by permission.

mentation, which have twice left bombs that failed to explode outside the home and under the car of University of California, Los Angeles (UCLA) animal researchers; another UCLA scientist had her home flooded. At the University of California, Berkeley and other Californian universities, professors, and even their children, are being harassed. According to a February 2008 article in the *San Francisco Chronicle* by Debra J. Saunders, these terror tactics are working and several scientists, fearful for their lives and those of their children, have given up doing research. The most terrifying part of her article is the following: "In 2005, Jerry Vlasak, a Southern California trauma surgeon and leader of the North American Animal Liberation Front, which is an animal rights organization, told a U.S. Senate committee that he could justify killing researchers. Vlasak said, 'I don't think you'd have to kill-assassinate too many. I think for five lives, 10 lives, 15 human lives, we could save 1 million, 2 million, or 10 million nonhuman lives.'" Of course, this kind of intimidation is not restricted to California. It is a problem for research institutions all over the United States and in the rest of the world.

Most people who oppose animal research are certainly not terrorists, and the fringe animal rights zealots, who can be found among the many kind, intelligent people in animal rights organizations, set back their cause by their extreme actions and statements. Many of the less extreme members of animal rights groups may actually condone experiments on animals, if they can be shown to help people. One problem is that it often takes a long time for the research and necessary follow-up experiments to be completed and critically evaluated before it can be determined whether any given avenue of research is going to provide a direct benefit to people—this is the very nature of all experimental biomedical research. Later in this [viewpoint], I will offer some of my own views on the benefits that have been derived from using animals as experimental models in biomedical research from the long-term perspective of nutrition science research, which I have been involved with during my many decades as a research scientist in nutritional biochemistry at the University of Wisconsin, Harvard University, and Tufts University.

Animals and Nutrition Research

A major premise of those who oppose animal experimentation is that it has done very little to improve human health. In my opinion, this position is untenable. Organizations that oppose the use of animals in medical research claim that few, if any, medical advances have resulted from animal experimentation. This is clearly untrue. The British Royal Society argues that virtually every medical achievement in the 20th century relied on the use of animals in some way. PETA (People for the Ethical Treatment of Animals), one of the largest and most influential anti-animal-experimentation organizations, posted on its website the following statement, which ought to be of interest to nutritionists:

> Medical historians have shown that improved nutrition and sanitary standards and other behavioral and environmental factors—rather than knowledge gained from animal experiments—are responsible for the decreasing number of deaths from common infectious diseases since 1900 and that medicine has had little to do with life expectancy.

The fact is that little was known about nutrition science before 1900. Prior to that time, it was believed that diets needed to contain proteins, carbohydrates, fats and minerals, but the necessary quality and quantity of these nutrients were unknown. The next half century, however, was particularly exciting for vitamin/nutrition research and a time in which appreciation of the usefulness of animal models in experimental nutrition research expanded.

Just prior to the dawn of the 20th century, a Dutch military doctor named [Christiaan] Eijkman, found that beriberi, a disease that debilitated and killed people by attacking their hearts and nervous systems, could be mimicked in some respects by feeding birds diets that were mainly composed of polished rice. The birds that were fed the polished rice developed polyneuritis and became paralyzed. However, Eijkman found that feeding rice still in the husk led to the bird's recovery. This observation led to further research that ended in the conclusion that a diet of over-milled rice was the chief cause of polyneuritis in birds and beriberi in man. In 1901, [Gerrit] Grijns extracted rice polishings with water and alcohol and, after feeding it to birds, concluded there was an essential nutrient—later to be identified as the B-vitamin thiamine—in the outer layers of rice that protected against beriberi. A whole new era in nutrition and medicine was started. . . .

The British Royal Society argues that virtually every medical achievement in the 20th century relied on the use of animals in some way.

A Greater Need for Animal Experimentation

For biomedical scientists this [the middle of the 20th century] was a very exciting time during which other essential nutrients, minerals, amino acids, and fatty acids were identified. The ways in which nutrients function and are metabolized were studied and the interrelationships of nutrients to one another were worked out. This was important because in real life nutritionally deficient people and animals are usually lacking in multiple essential nutrients. Many metabolic enzymatic pathways require a number of micronutrients to work together. Much of this metabolic information was obtained through animal experimentation.

I have used examples from 20th-century vitamin history to illustrate the impact of animal research on important nutritional discoveries and to show that, contrary to what PETA claims, animal nutrition studies since 1900 have saved or enhanced the lives of millions of humans. Those who oppose the use of animals say that alternative scientific methods can achieve the same or better results. They suggest that epidemiological studies, in vitro studies, cell and tissue studies, clinical studies, computer modeling, and scans can be used. These methods of investigation all provide useful information and the search for alternatives to animal experimentation is a priority at the National Institutes of Health, at American universities, and at medical research organizations throughout the world. I doubt, however, that the need for animal studies will disappear. In fact, from what little I know about modern molecular biology and genetics, I would not be surprised if there will soon be an increased need for animal experimentation in order to truly understand the secrets of our DNA.

I doubt ... that the need for animal studies will disappear.

The Biomedical Needs of Animals

Animal rights advocates are against the practice of pet food manufacturers testing their foods on animals. In the United States, in order to make nutritional claims for pet foods, such as the ability of a food to sustain growth and maintenance or reproduction, experimental evidence is required to support the claim. There is also the obvious need to determine whether the animal foods are palatable. To get this information, aren't animal studies needed?

Animals are living creatures and thus develop various diseases. If, as animal rights groups say the medical problems of humans ought to be studied on people then it seems that the problems of animals ought to be researched on animals. However, in reading the literature produced by animal rights organizations, I have been impressed by the complete lack of discussion on how to do research on the biomedical needs of animals. The potential value of this type of experimental work on animals can be illustrated from some of my own early professional work in nutrition.

As a graduate student at the University of Wisconsin, I worked with a group of other scientists on a serious problem of dogs. At that time, in 1947, a mysterious disease had killed 75,000 dogs in Chicago. The disease, called "running fits" in the United States and "canine hysteria" in Great Britain had been known about for more than 15 years, and a year earlier the famous British scientist [Edward] Mellanby had associated it with the consumption by dogs of wheat flour treated with a protein-maturing chemical called agene (nitrogen trichloride). Agene was used in the milling process because agene-treated flour made better bread. Eighty-five percent of the flour milled at that time in the United States, Britain, and Belgium was treated with agene. The afflicted dogs showed electroencephalographs similar to those seen in epileptics, so understanding the problem of running fits in dogs had possible ramifications for people. It turned out that agene oxidized the amino acid methionine to a previously unknown type of compound (methionine sulfoximine) that caused the disease. Moreover, we found that sensitivity to the agent varied markedly in various species of animals, with humans being very resistant. As a result of this work, the use of agene in the milling industry was halted and the lives of countless numbers of dogs were saved. It was not pleasant doing this kind of experimental work with dogs, but I believe it was necessary, and it clearly had a lifesaving outcome.

The experimental studies we did with cats clearly led to a lifesaving outcome for large numbers of cats.

Human and Animal Health Can Go Hand in Hand

When I completed my graduate studies at Wisconsin, I joined the Department of Nutrition at the Harvard School of Public Health. Shortly after I arrived in Boston, an official arrived from StarKist Foods. They produced cat foods under the label

Nine Lives. They and other cat food manufacturers made some of their canned foods from red tuna meat. The cats loved it to the exclusion of other foods, with the result that they developed a disease called steatitis or yellow fat disease. The fat of these cats became yellow and lumpy. They were in pain, developed fevers, and died. There was very little known about cat nutrition at the time and I agreed to work on the problem of steatitis. The steatitis problem turned out to be a vitamin E deficiency caused by low vitamin E and very large quantities of polyunsaturated fatty acids in red tuna meat, specifically vascular tissue in tuna. Many commercial cat foods now contain added vitamin E. The experimental studies we did with cats clearly led to a lifesaving outcome for large numbers of cats.

Upon my arrival in Boston, I also found that a group of cats was being studied, which had developed severely damaged kidneys that contained considerable amounts of crystalline material. With the help of Harvard's geology department, which had X-ray diffraction equipment, we learned that the material was calcium oxalate. Oxalate is not metabolized in animals, and it was thought that it was not synthesized in animals either. As a result, biochemists were not interested in it. However, physicians were interested because two-thirds of human kidney stones contain either calcium oxalate alone or in combination with other minerals. It was thought that the oxalate that humans excrete came from plant sources. It turned out that the cats we had were vitamin B6 deficient and they were synthesizing oxalate. Chemical analysis showed that the commercial cat food we were using was loaded with vitamin B6, but it was not biologically available. In order to study this problem further, we switched from cats to rats and soon found we were able to produce kidney stones in rats that were similar in composition to those seen in people. Further studies indicated that increasing the magnesium content of the rat's diets prevented stones from forming. We then studied people with histories of recurrent oxalate stone formation and found that by supplementing their magnesium intake, we could keep them from making new stones. It is hard to express the pleasure I felt with this accomplishment based on animal experiments. . . .

People who have animal pets or who use them in their work have legal and moral obligations to not unnecessarily hurt or abuse them.

Animal Rights and Humane Treatment

The animal rights people believe that much of the research conducted using animals is without merit and is done simply to satisfy the investigator's curiosity. I cannot believe that any research in any field is not motivated by curiosity. However, animal experiments are very costly, and for scientists to convince their institutions and granting agencies to support the work, it needs to have merit. A fundamental belief of animal rights extremists is that animals have rights similar to those of people. I do not believe that animals have rights. However, as an animal lover, I strongly believe that people who have animal pets or who use them in their work have legal and moral obligations to not unnecessarily hurt or abuse them. I also believe that all animals are not equal. I think that sub-human primates, especially the large apes are unique and require special care if they have to be used in experiments. I would never knowingly work with an animal that had been somebody's pet. I am amazed that, until recently, many people did not believe that animals experience pain and many academics do not believe that animals have feelings.

Considering the large numbers of people and institutions engaged in animal experimentation, it would be surprising if there were not some instances of animal abuse. In many places, animal caretakers are paid minimum wages and are given inadequate instructions. Government inspection agencies are also poorly staffed. Private and public agencies do a wonderful job of caring for lost and mistreated animals. I never realized how large a problem ill treatment of animals is until I started to watch Animal Planet on television. Recently, the government ordered the seizure of 140 million pounds of beef, packed in a plant in California where sick cows were abused and slaughtered. The discovery of this shameful situation was made by the Humane Society [of the United States], not by federal or state meat inspectors at the plant. In my experience, the people who work for organizations like the Humane Society are animal lovers who are smart, caring, and dedicated to protecting animals. The zealots who can be found among the many kind, intelligent people in animal rights organizations set back their cause by their extreme actions and their extreme statements. What sane person, for example, could possibly support the recent statement of PETA that [it] would not support an experiment that would sacrifice 10 animals to save the lives of 10,000 people?

Japan's Cultural Traditions Shape Its Animal Experimentation Policies

Hiromi Takahashi-Omoe and Katsuhiko Omoe

Hiromi Takahashi-Omoe is a scientist at the National Institute of Science and Technology Policy in Japan, and Katsuhiko Omoe is a scientist in the Department of Veterinary Medicine at Iwate University in Japan. In the following viewpoint, they challenge the belief that Japan's system of regulating animal experimentation is not strict enough because it is self-regulated. According to the authors, Japanese practices regarding animals are heavily influenced by culture, religion, and tradition—specifically aspects of Buddhism. While the system is not perfect, it continues to serve people and animals well.

As you read, consider the following questions:

1. What are the 5Rs?
2. Why do the authors say the Japanese hold memorial services for sacrificed animals?
3. What are the two types of guidelines specific to animal experimentation in Japan?

Hiromi Takahashi-Omoe and Katsuhiko Omoe, "Japanese Policy on Animal Welfare: An Instructive Example for Scientific Animal Experimentation," *Annual Review of Biomedical Sciences*, vol. 10, 2008, pp. 64–65, 67–70, 75. Copyright © 2008 by *Annual Review of Biomedical Sciences*. Reproduced by permission.

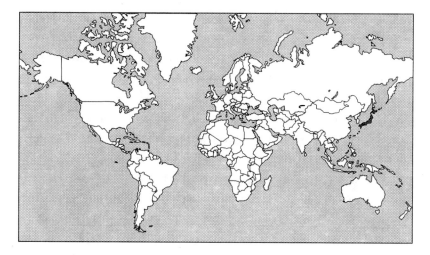

Animal use for scientific purposes, 'animal experimentation', is conducible to scientific development, protecting human health, civilized way of life and so on; however, animal use for human advantage is controversial. Despite the heated discussion on the rights and wrongs of experimentation, animals have been used for research, testing and education in many nations under management systems for the appropriate use of animals from both scientific and ethical viewpoints. Previous efforts to achieve a delicate balance between the scientific rationale and animal protection involve the welfare of animals in scientific procedures.

The management systems of animal experimentation vary among nations, some based on legislation on the protection of animals used for experimental and other scientific purposes, others on peer review or other forms of non-legislated overseeing, and yet others on a combination of legislated and non-legislated overseeing. In Japan, each institution where animal experimentation is conducted (hereinafter, institution) independently regulates its use of animals under the Ministry's fundamental guidelines, without legal binding force. The management systems are so-called 'self-regulated' or 'self-motivated management'. In all nations, the management systems for animal experimentation are based on the international basic principles of humane experimental techniques for laboratory animals, the 'three Rs' tenet of replacement, reduction, and refinement of animal usage or the 'five Rs' of the 3Rs plus responsibility and review (hereinafter, 3Rs or 5Rs). The 3Rs or 5Rs are currently recognized as the measures for animal welfare in scientific procedures and are applied to animal experimentation around the world.

As described above, Japan has regulated animal experimentation based on self-motivated management systems. These management systems have continued without any critical problems; however, they have acquired a reputation for being opaque by other nations. Unfortunately, Japan has long been misunderstood to not have consistent management systems for animal experimentation. This misunderstanding seems to have been resolved by enforcing the Ministry's fundamental guidelines for animal experimentation in 2006; however, it should be kept in mind that Japan has long managed experimentation without any severe mishaps, even before introducing the Ministry's fundamental guidelines. Japan has a policy of promoting self-motivated management systems for animal experimentation without strict laws and regulations and treats the Ministry's fundamental guidelines as a measure for executing these systems. . . .

Unfortunately, Japan has long been misunderstood to not have consistent management systems for animal experimentation.

The Legislation Process for Animal Experimentation in Japan

In the course of establishing a concept for the treatment and management of animals, Japanese included their religions, traditions and regulatory and administrative frameworks of science and technology, and adopted the ideas and actions of other nations. Generally, it is considered that Japanese ideas of the relationship between humans and animals have been affected by Buddhism, which has been tightly linked with 'animism' and has been adopted in Japan. These features are described below.

- Guilt for killing and wounding animals, which is based on the tradition of 'ahimsa';

- The idea that humans and animals are equal from the viewpoint of existence, which is based on the tradition that Buddha's soul dwells in all earthly things;

- The idea that human life is linked to animal life, which is based on the tradition of transmigration (samsara).

As described above, Japanese embrace the idea of transmigration between humans and animals; however, they consider that humans and animals are not ranked equally and that humans are always dominant over animals. This people-centered idea is symbolized by the Japanese thought that humans might descend downward (transmigrate) to a lower form of being, such as an animal, if they commit many wrongful acts.

The above ideas, influenced by Buddhism, have been perpetuated among the Japanese and have affected their emotional response to animals. Based on these ideas, the Japanese justify the use and killing of animals for their advantage and hold memorial services for sacrificed animals, incorporating methods to reduce their feelings of guilt about animal use. This established practice has also been introduced into animal experimentation; for example, most Japanese institutions where experimentation is performed currently hold voluntary memorial services for laboratory animals every year.

The legislation for animal experimentation has been established according to the above ideas and by adjusting the related regulations to prevent abuse, for protection, humane treatment and management of animals. . . .

The law defines animal experimentation as the 'utilization of animals for education, testing, research and development, manufacture of biological products, or other scientific purposes' and requires the humane treatment of animals based on the 3Rs.

Under the 'Law for the Humane Treatment and Management of Animals', the 'Fundamental National Policy on Animal Treatment' was stipulated in 2006 to disseminate the concept of the law throughout Japan. The policy clearly specifies the Japanese concept of animal welfare as described below.

> We are beings that live by using other living beings and sacrificing their life; therefore, we should not deny that we have to use and sacrifice animals for our survival and should gravely accept animal use in our life as a natural act in the order of life. However, we must not trivialize the lives of animals or use animals unnecessarily. It is necessary to cultivate respect for life, feeling of fellowship, and peace in our society, as described in the purpose of the 'Law for the Humane Treatment and Management of Animals', to pay respect to the lives of animals and treat animals humanely.

This description in the National Policy, encompassing animal welfare, is generally applicable to all Japanese people. The concept also offers a rationale for conducting animal experimentation in Japan. . . .

Current Management Systems

The law, policy, standards and guidelines have a basic role in the conduct of animal experimentation; however, they cannot legally restrict experimentation. The Japanese management of animal experimentation is based on a system strongly reflecting the responsibility of each institution and animal experimenter, such as researchers in the institution; therefore, the Japanese system involves a so-called 'self-motivated management' or 'self-regulation' of animal experimentation. . . .

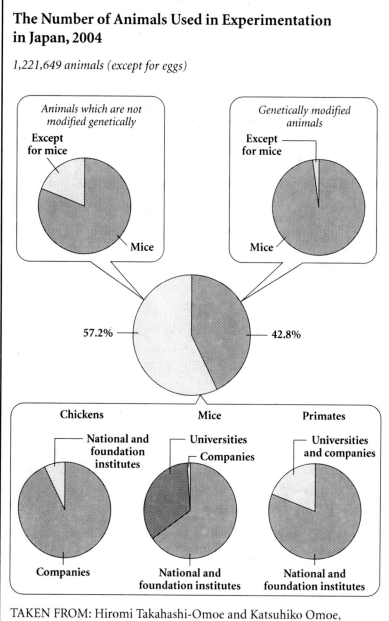

The Number of Animals Used in Experimentation in Japan, 2004

1,221,649 animals (except for eggs)

Animals which are not modified genetically

Except for mice

Mice

Genetically modified animals

Except for mice

Mice

57.2% — — 42.8%

Chickens

National and foundation institutes

Companies

Mice

Universities

Companies

National and foundation institutes

Primates

Universities and companies

National and foundation institutes

TAKEN FROM: Hiromi Takahashi-Omoe and Katsuhiko Omoe, "Japanese Policy on Animal Welfare: An Instructive Example for Scientific Animal Experimentation," *Annual Review of Biomedical Sciences*, vol. 10, 2008.

Depending on the purpose of experimentation, it may be subject to several laws, such as the 'Pharmaceutical Law' that regulates animal testing for medicines, and the ministerial ordinance for experimentation using genetically modified animals under the 'Law Concerning the Conservation and Sustainable Use of Biological Diversity Through Regulations on the Use of Living Modified Organisms', which was formulated to ensure the precise and straightforward implementation of the Cartagena Protocol on Biosafety that Japan ratified in November 2003. However, these have been not integrated into a single comprehensive law with overall control of animal experimentation in Japan. . . .

Guidelines . . . require experiments to have a fine balance between the scientific rationale and animal welfare.

There are two kinds of guidelines specific to animal experimentation in Japan: the fundamental guidelines formulated by the related ministries and the practical guidelines by the Science Council of Japan. The former fundamental guidelines have a central role in managing animal experimentation. Although the guidelines are formulated and managed independently by 3 ministries, the basic policy is common, as a matter of course. The fundamental guidelines were formulated independently by these ministries because they can work out details of their content, depending on the variety of purposes of animal experimentation. In the fundamental guidelines, animal experimentation is defined as described below.

'Animal experiments and related activities are necessary and unavoidable for gaining scientific insight into the biological activities of living organisms, but they must be performed properly, taking into consideration the welfare of animals' (preamble to the guidelines). The guidelines therefore require experiments to have a fine balance between the scientific rationale and animal welfare.

Institutions Take Responsibility for Animal Welfare

The guidelines define the framework for self-motivated management systems of animal experimentation by each institution, which involves living mammalian, avian and reptilian species, but not amphibians, fish and dead animals. The framework of the guidelines consists of the responsibilities of the director of each institution, including the establishment of institutional regulations and the approval of protocols for each animal experiment, the establishment of an institutional animal care and use committee, special attention to the conduct of animal experimentation, the rearing and maintenance of laboratory animals, and the provisions of education and training relating to animal experimentation, self-inspections and evaluation of compliance with the guidelines, external verification of the results of the self-inspections and self-evaluations, and public disclosure of information regarding the conduct of animal experimentation.

The latter practical guidelines formulated by the Science Council of Japan maintain consistency with the above fundamental guidelines and serve as reference material and a model when institutions compile their own specifications for animal experimentation according to the Ministry's fundamental guidelines. . . .

These systems . . . are appropriate for Japanese religions, traditions and regulatory and administrative frameworks.

The above fundamental and practical guidelines for animal experimentation have set out the basic concept for compliance in every institution. Under these guidelines, the director of each institution sets out unique internal regulations to manage their own experimentation (hereafter, institutional regulations), introducing useful foreign references such as the 'Categories of Biomedical Experiments Based on Increasing

Ethical Concerns for Non-human Species' formulated by the Scientists Center for Animal Welfare (SCAW), which improves animal experimentation from the viewpoint of 'refinement' in the 3Rs. Almost all institutions have their own regulations and have revised them according to the fundamental and practical guidelines, if needed. . . .

Japan has set up self-motivated management systems for animal experimentation without strict laws and regulations. These systems are unique, a departure from those in the EU [European Union], US and Canada, and are appropriate for Japanese religions, traditions and regulatory and administrative frameworks of science and technology. These management systems will continue; however, operation of the systems will be revised through trial and error, depending on the domestic and international environment. In order to implement appropriate animal care, use and management in future scientific procedures, not only animal experimenters but also people who benefit from animal experimentation must develop common perceptions of animal welfare through discussion because it is difficult to uniformly assess animal experimentation from the standpoint of animal welfare in the current situation, although experimentation can be assessed scientifically. From this regard, we hope that our report will be helpful to build consensus about animal welfare in scientific procedures.

Studying Pet Dogs with Cancer Can Help Humans Around the World

David J. Waters and Kathleen Wildasin

David J. Waters is a professor of comparative oncology at Purdue University, and Kathleen Wildasin is a Kentucky-based medical and science writer. In the following viewpoint, they argue that pet dogs can be used to advance treatments and even find a cure for certain kinds of cancers in humans. Waters and Wildasin assert that studying pet dogs with cancer can also lead to more knowledge about causes of cancer and even cancer prevention. They are not advocating giving healthy dogs cancer but studying already sick dogs in the hopes of gaining valuable insight.

As you read, consider the following questions:

1. According to the viewpoint, what fraction of American households own dogs?
2. What does ATN-161 do in the treatment of cancer?
3. What does "chemoprevention" mean, in the authors' view?

Imagine a 60-year-old man recuperating at home after prostate cancer surgery, drawing comfort from the aged golden retriever beside him. This man might know that a few years

David J. Waters and Kathleen Wildasin, "Cancer Clues from Pet Dogs," *Scientific American*, December 2006, pp. 95–96, 98–101. Copyright © 2006 by *Scientific American* a division of Nature America, Inc. All rights reserved. Reproduced with permission.

ago the director of the National Cancer Institute issued a challenge to cancer researchers, urging them to find ways to "eliminate the suffering and death caused by cancer by 2015." What he probably does not realize, though, is that the pet at his side could be an important player in that effort.

Pet dogs and humans are the only two species that naturally develop lethal prostate cancers.

Reaching the ambitious Cancer 2015 goal will require the application of everything in investigators' tool kits, including an openness to new ideas. Despite an unprecedented surge in researchers' understanding of what cancer cells can do, the translation of this knowledge into saving lives has been unacceptably slow. Investigators have discovered many drugs that cure artificially induced cancers in rodents, but when the substances move into human trials, they usually have rough sledding. The rodent models called on to mimic human cancers are just not measuring up. If we are going to beat cancer, we need a new path to progress.

Now consider these facts. More than a third of American households include dogs, and scientists estimate that some four million of these animals will be diagnosed with cancer this year. Pet dogs and humans are the only two species that naturally develop lethal prostate cancers. The type of breast cancer that affects pet dogs spreads preferentially to bones—just as it does in women. And the most frequent bone cancer of pet dogs, osteosarcoma, is the same cancer that strikes teenagers.

Researchers in the emerging field of comparative oncology believe such similarities offer a novel approach for combating the cancer problem. These investigators compare naturally occurring cancers in animals and people—exploring their striking resemblances as well as their notable differences.

Right now comparative oncologists are enlisting pet dogs to tackle the very obstacles that stand in the way of achieving the Cancer 2015 goal. Among the issues on their minds are finding better treatments, deciding which doses of medicines will work best, identifying environmental factors that trigger cancer development, understanding why some individuals are resistant to malignancies and figuring out how to prevent cancer. As the Cancer 2015 clock keeps ticking, comparative oncologists ask, Why not transform the cancer toll in pet dogs from something that is only a sorrow today into a national resource, both for helping other pets and for aiding people?

Why Rover?

For decades, scientists have tested the toxicity of new cancer agents on laboratory beagles before studying the compounds in humans. Comparative oncologists have good reason to think that pet dogs with naturally occurring cancers can likewise become good models for testing the antitumor punch delivered by promising treatments.

One reason has to do with the way human trials are conducted. Because of the need to ensure that the potential benefits of an experimental therapy outweigh the risks, researchers end up evaluating drugs with the deck stacked against success; they attempt to thrash bulky, advanced cancers that have failed previous treatment with other agents. In contrast, comparative oncologists can test new treatment ideas against early-stage cancers—delivering the drugs just as they would ultimately be used in people. When experimental drugs prove helpful in pets, researchers gain a leg up on knowing which therapies are most likely to aid human patients. So comparative oncologists are optimistic that their findings in dogs will be more predictive than rodent studies have been and will help expeditiously identify those agents that should (and should not) be tested in large-scale human trials.

Pet dogs can reveal much about human cancers in part because of the animals' tendency to become afflicted with the same types of malignancies that affect people. Examples abound. The most frequently diagnosed form of lymphoma affecting dogs mimics the medium- and high-grade B cell non-Hodgkin's lymphomas in people. Osteosarcoma, the most common bone cancer of large- and giant-breed dogs, closely resembles the osteosarcoma in teenagers in its skeletal location and aggressiveness. Under a microscope, cancer cells from a teenager with osteosarcoma are indistinguishable from a golden retriever's bone cancer cells. Bladder cancer, melanoma and mouth cancer are other examples plaguing both dog and master. In a different kind of similarity, female dogs spayed before puberty are less prone to breast cancer than are their non-spayed counterparts, much as women who have their ovaries removed, who begin to menstruate late or who go into menopause early have a reduced risk for breast cancer.

Under a microscope, cancer cells from a teenager with osteosarcoma are indistinguishable from a golden retriever's bone cancer cells.

Canine cancers also mimic those of humans in another attribute—metastasis, the often life-threatening spread of cancer cells to distant sites throughout the body. Solving the mystery of how tumor cells metastasize to particular organs is a top research priority. When certain types of cancers spread to distant organs, they tend to go preferentially to some tissues over others, for reasons that are not entirely clear. Because metastasis is what accounts for most deaths from cancer, researchers would very much like to gain a better understanding of its controls. Studies in pet dogs with prostate or breast cancer might prove particularly useful in this effort, because such tumors frequently spread in dogs as they do in humans—to the skeleton. Indeed, research in pet dogs is already attempting to

work out the interactions between tumor cells and bone that make the skeleton such a favorite site for colonization.

Scientists also have deeper theoretical grounds for thinking that pet dogs are reasonable models for human cancer. Evolutionary biologists note that dogs and humans are built like Indy racecars, with successful reproduction as the finish line. We are designed to win the race, but afterward it does not matter how rapidly we fall apart. This design makes us ill equipped to resist or repair the genetic damage that accumulates in our bodies. Eventually this damage can derange cells enough to result in cancer. In the distant past, our human ancestors did not routinely live long enough to become afflicted with age-related cancers. But modern sanitation and medicine have rendered both longevity and cancer in old age common. Much the same is true for our pets. Pet dogs, whom we carefully protect from predation and disease, live longer than their wild ancestors did and so become prone to cancer in their later years. Thus, when it comes to a high lifetime risk for cancer, pets and people are very much in the same boat.

When it comes to a high lifetime risk for cancer, pets and people are very much in the same boat.

Aside from acquiring cancers that resemble those in people, pet dogs are valuable informants for other reasons. Compared with humans, they have compressed life spans, so scientists can more quickly determine whether a new prevention strategy or therapy has a good chance of improving human survival rates. Finally, although veterinarians today are far better equipped to treat cancer than they used to be, the standard treatments for many canine tumors remain ineffective. Because most pet cancer diagnoses end in death, dog owners are often eager to enroll their animals in clinical trials that could save their pet's life—and possibly provide the necessary evidence to move a promising therapy to human clinical trials.

Advancing Cancer Therapy

Various cancer treatment studies featuring pet dogs have now been carried out or begun. Some of the earliest work focused on saving the limbs of teenagers with bone cancer. Twenty-five years ago a diagnosis of osteosarcoma in a youngster meant amputation of the affected limb, ineffective or no chemotherapy (drugs administered into the bloodstream to attack tumors anywhere in the body), and almost certain death. Today limb amputation can be avoided by chiseling out the diseased bone tissue and replacing it with a bone graft and metal implant—a process partially perfected in pet dogs by Stephen Withrow and his colleagues at Colorado State University. Withrow's team pioneered technical advances that reduced the likelihood of complications, such as placing bone cement in the marrow space of the bone graft. The researchers also showed that preoperative chemotherapy delivered directly into an artery could convert an inoperable tumor into an operable one. The group's work is credited with significantly increasing the percentage of teenagers who today can be cured of osteosarcoma.

Although a tumor's local effects are often controllable using surgery or radiation, metastasis is much harder to combat. For that, drug therapy is required. New compounds under development aim to disrupt key cellular events that regulate the survival and proliferation of metastatic tumor deposits as well as their sensitivity to cancer-fighting drugs. One experimental agent, ATN-161, which inhibits the formation of new blood vessels that foster tumor growth and metastasis, is currently being evaluated in large-breed dogs with bone cancers that have spread to the lungs. The ability of ATN-161 to enhance the effects of conventional chemotherapies is also under study. If these trials succeed, they could smooth the way toward clinical trials in humans.

Cancer researchers are also turning their attention to more familiar kinds of pharmaceuticals, including nonsteroidal anti-

inflammatory drugs (NSAIDs), the class of compounds that includes ibuprofen. Certain NSAIDs have exhibited significant antitumor activity against a variety of canine tumors. In studies of pet dogs with bladder cancer, for example, the NSAID piroxicam showed such impressive antitumor activity that the drug is now in human clinical trials to see if this treatment can derail the progression of precancerous bladder lesions to life-threatening cancer.

Developing new cancer therapies is not just about finding novel drugs. It is about optimizing drug delivery to the patient. In your vein or up your nose? That is the kind of information scientists testing new agents against lung cancer need to know. If the right amount of drug does not make it to the tumor, then even substances with impressive credentials for killing tumor cells in a Petri dish will not stand a chance of working in human patients. Moreover, delivering pharmaceuticals directly to the target—so-called regional therapy—has the added benefit of avoiding the toxicity associated with systemic therapy.

Investigators have used pet dogs to study the intranasal delivery of a cytokine, a small immune system molecule, called interleukin-2 (IL-2) to treat naturally occurring lung cancers. Positive results from these experiments led to feasibility trials of inhaled IL-2 in human patients with lung metastases, further leading to trials with another cytokine, granulocyte colony-stimulating factor. Pet dogs can also aid researchers in optimizing the dosing and delivery protocols for drugs that have already made their way into human trials.

Pet dogs are helping optimize the next generation of technologies for improved cancer detection.

Another challenge that pet dogs are helping to overcome is determining the extent of tumor spread, called clinical staging. Accurate staging is critical for devising therapeutic game plans that will maximally benefit the patient while minimizing exposure to harsh treatments that are unlikely to help at a given disease stage. For example, the odds that a teenager will survive osteosarcoma are increased by accurate identification (and subsequent surgical removal) of lung metastases.

Doctors typically determine the presence and extent of such metastases with noninvasive imaging techniques, such as computed tomography (CT). To assess how accurate such scanning is, one of us (Waters), along with investigators from Indiana University School of Medicine, collected CT images of the lungs from pet dogs with metastatic bone cancer and then examined the tissue at autopsy to verify that what was interpreted as a "tumor" on the scan really was a tumor and not a mistake. Results showed that state-of-the-art imaging with CT—the same type used in clinical staging of bone cancer in teenagers—significantly underestimates the number of cancer deposits within the lung. By revealing the limited accuracy of existing and experimental techniques, pet dogs are helping optimize the next generation of technologies for improved cancer detection.

Taking Aim at Cancer Prevention

But cancer researchers are shooting for more than improved detection and better treatment; they also want to prevent the disease. Surprisingly, prevention is a relatively new concept within the cancer research community. What cardiologists have known for a long time—that millions of lives can be saved through the prevention of heart disease—is just now gaining traction in the cancer field. The term "chemoprevention" was coined 30 years ago to refer to the administration of compounds to prevent cancer, but scientists did not gather nationally to debate cutting-edge knowledge of cancer prevention until October 2002.

Today the pace is quickening as investigators are examining a diverse armamentarium of potential cancer-protective

The Importance of SIV Studies

Over the past few years, studies of SIV [simian immunodeficiency virus] infection in natural African NHP [nonhuman primate] hosts have provided crucial benchmarks to critically evaluate some of the core paradigms of AIDS [acquired immune deficiency syndrome] pathogenesis. Clearly, this work has demonstrated that understanding the mechanisms by which natural SIV hosts avoid AIDS is essential to identifying correlates of protection from disease progression during HIV [human immunodeficiency virus] infection. The occurrence of a handful of cases of AIDS in natural hosts, whose presentation is very similar to that observed in pathogenic HIV and SIV infections, indicates that the lack of disease progression is actively achieved by natural SIV hosts. This conclusion further emphasizes the importance of studying SIV infections in African NHPs as models of effective control of disease progression. Importantly, this type of AIDS resistance is independent of immunological control of virus replication and, in some instances, even independent of preservation of $CD4^+$ T cell homeostasis. Understanding the mechanisms by which natural hosts regularly avoid disease progression upon SIV infection will have profound implications in terms of HIV/AIDS pathogenesis, therapy, and vaccines.

Ivona Pandrea, Guido Silvestri, and Cristian Apetrei,
"AIDS in African Nonhuman Primate Hosts of SIVs:
A New Paradigm of SIV Infection,"
Current HIV Research, *vol. 7, 2009.*

agents. But finding the proper dose of promising agents has always been challenging. Indeed, failure to do so proved disastrous for some early human trials of preventives. For example, in two large lung cancer prevention trials, people receiving high doses of the antioxidant nutrient beta-carotene had an unexpected *increase* in lung cancer incidence compared with placebo-treated control subjects.

Can dogs accelerate progress in cancer prevention? Recently canine studies have helped define the dose of an antioxidant—the trace mineral selenium—that minimizes cancer-causing genetic damage within the aging prostate. The message from the dogs: When it comes to taking dietary supplements such as selenium to reduce your cancer risk, more of a good thing is not necessarily better. Elderly dogs given moderate doses ended up with less DNA damage in their prostates than dogs given lower or higher amounts. Comparative oncologists hold that dog studies conducted before large-scale human prevention trials are initiated can streamline the process of finding the most effective dose of cancer preventives and can enable oncologists to lob a well-aimed grenade at the cancer foe.

Pet dogs can assist in preventing human cancers in another way. For years, dogs in the research laboratory have advanced understanding of the acute and long-term effects of high doses of cancer-causing chemicals. But pet dogs, just by going about their daily lives, could serve as sentinels—watchdogs, if you will—to identify substances in our homes and in our backyards that are carcinogenic at lower doses. If something can cause cancer, the disease will show up in pets, with their compressed life spans, well before it will in people.

Take asbestos. Most human cases of mesothelioma (a malignancy of tissues lining the chest and abdomen) stem from asbestos exposure. Symptoms can appear up to 30 years after the incriminating exposure. Investigators have now documented that mesothelioma in pet dogs is also largely related to encountering asbestos, most likely through being near a master who came into contact with it through a hobby or work. But in dogs, the time between exposure and diagnosis is comparatively brief—less than eight years. So the appearance of the cancer in a dog can alert people to look for and remediate any remaining sources of asbestos. Also, closer monitoring of exposed individuals might lead to earlier diagnosis of mesothelioma and render these cancers curable.

Pet dogs could assist in discovering other environmental hazards. Some well-documented geographic "hot spots" show an unusually high incidence of certain cancers. For example, women living in Marin County, California, have the country's highest breast cancer rate. Scientists typically try to identify the factors contributing to cancer in hot spots by comparing the genetics and behavior of people who become afflicted and those who do not. To advance the effort, comparative oncologists are now establishing cancer registries for pet dogs in those areas. If both pets and people living in a particular community experience higher-than-normal cancer rates, the finding would strengthen suspicions that these malignancies are being triggered by something in the environment.

If something can cause cancer, the disease will show in pets, with their compressed life spans, well before it will in people.

Analyzing tissues of dogs could even potentially speed identification of the specific hazard. Many toxic chemicals, such as pesticides, concentrate themselves in body fat. So it might make sense to collect tissues from dogs during common elective surgical procedures (for example, spaying) or at autopsy. Later, if an unusually high number of people in an area acquire a certain form of cancer, investigators could analyze levels of different chemicals in the samples to see if any are particularly prominent and worth exploring as a contributing factor.

Why Uncle Bill Avoided Cancer

Because cancer in pet dogs is so commonplace, the animals might be able to assist in solving an age-old mystery. Almost everyone has an Uncle Bill who smoked two packs a day and never got lung cancer. So what factors determine cancer resistance? One way to tease out the answer is to find populations resistant to cancer and study them closely—their genetics, their diet and their lifestyle.

Such a population has been found—human centenarians. It turns out that most folks who live to be 100 die of disorders other than cancer. But it is nearly impossible to collect reliable information from a 102-year-old woman on her dietary habits and physical activity when she was a teenager or in her mid-40s. So one of us (Waters) asked a simple question: Is this phenomenon of cancer resistance in the oldest old operational in pet dogs? The answer is yes. Now by interviewing owners of very old pet dogs, comparative oncologists can construct accurate lifetime histories of "centenarian" dogs. Combine this prospect with the ability to collect biological samples (such as blood for genetic analysis and for tests of organ function) from very old dogs as well as from several generations of their offspring, and you have a unique field laboratory for probing the genetic and environmental determinants of cancer resistance.

The puzzle of cancer resistance can also be addressed in another way—by examining differences in cancer susceptibility between dogs and humans. In people, obesity and diets rich in animal fat are known to increase risk for colon cancer. In contrast, colorectal cancer in dogs is uncommon, even though many pet dogs are obese and consume a high-fat diet. Scientists are now contemplating the use of dogs as a "negative model" of colon cancer in the hope of identifying factors able to confer cancer resistance to people whose style of living strongly favors colon cancer development. Knowledge of resistance factors could suggest new interventions for nonresistant individuals.

A Growing Effort

Historically, comparative oncology research has been conducted in university-based hospitals and laboratories where veterinary oncologists are trained. But other organizations have begun to recognize the potential for this kind of research to translate into better care for people, and these institutions are now actively engaged in comparative oncology research.

The Gerald P. Murphy Cancer Foundation began in 2001 to accelerate the discovery of improved methods for preventing and treating prostate and bone cancers affecting both people and pets. The Animal Cancer Foundation in New York City has funded comparative oncology studies and has recently established a repository of biological specimens of diseased and healthy animals as a resource for researchers chasing biological indicators of cancer risk. And in 2003 the National Cancer Institute developed the Comparative Oncology Program, which designs trials involving dogs with naturally occurring cancers and also provides researchers with high-quality, canine-specific reagents needed for in-depth studies of the molecular biology, protein chemistry and genetics of dog tumors.

No single, ideal animal model for cancer exists.

Moreover, the sequencing of the canine genome is now complete. Discovery that a particular gene is involved in some form of cancer in dogs will enable investigators to determine whether—and how—the same gene operates in human cancers. Scottish terriers with bladder cancer, rottweilers with bone cancer and golden retrievers with lymphoma—each breed can help elucidate the calamitous combinations of genes and environment that lead to cancer.

Of course, there are limitations inherent in the use of animals to mimic human cancer—whether you are talking about rodents, dogs or other species. No single, ideal animal model for cancer exists. The best science is done by asking good questions and then using the research tools most likely to yield meaningful answers. At times, following that rule in cancer research will mean turning to dogs to track down that hard-to-win knowledge.

The intriguing similarities between the cancers of people and pets—once a mere curiosity—are now being systematically applied to transform cancer from killer to survivable nuisance. Comparative oncologists are not inducing cancer in animals but are compassionately treating pet dogs suffering from the same kinds of lethal cancers that develop naturally in both man and man's best friend. They are putting our canine companions on the trail of a killer in ways that can save both pets and people.

The European Union's Cosmetics Directive Has Many Loopholes

Uncaged Campaigns

Uncaged Campaigns is a United Kingdom–based nonprofit organization that seeks to protect the rights of animals across the globe. In the following viewpoint, the group argues that the European Union's Cosmetics Directive is flawed. The directive is due to be enforced in 2013 and will ban the sale of cosmetics tested on animals throughout the European Union. However, Uncaged Campaigns asserts that loopholes exist that will allow companies to continue to use animals in product testing. In addition, Uncaged Campaigns insists that the British government is involved in these deceptions.

As you read, consider the following questions:

1. When is the complete sales ban on cosmetics tested on animals due to be enforced in the European Union?

2. About how many animals does Uncaged Campaigns estimate could be saved in the EU from poisoning tests of cosmetics if the ban is enforced?

3. What is the Cosmetic Products (Safety) Regulations 2008, as Uncaged Campaigns describes?

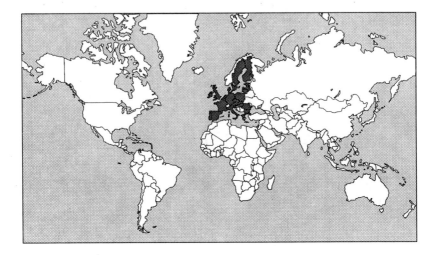

March 11, 2009, should mark a momentous day in the history of the anti-vivisection movement, but legal loopholes and Government indifference threaten to perpetuate the most gratuitous and extreme forms of animal cruelty. After a decades-long fight, two key Europe-wide measures to tackle animal testing are due to come into force as part of the EU's [European Union's] 'Cosmetics Directive':

1. a ban on animal testing of cosmetics ingredients ('Cosmetics' has a wide legal definition here and includes toiletries)

2. a ban on the sale of cosmetic products and ingredients tested on animals anywhere in the world for all but three test areas, regardless of the availability of alternative nonanimal tests

The complete sales ban where no animal tests are allowed at all for cosmetics sold in the EU is due to kick in during 2013. It is widely believed that the bans, supposed to [be] enforced irrespective of the availability of validated 'alternatives', [have] provided a serious incentive for companies to invest in nonanimal, advanced testing methods.

Too Soon to Celebrate

The latest annual EU figures suggest that over 5,500 animals could be saved from poisoning tests for cosmetics in the EU alone, never mind the global impact as companies stop animal testing in order to continue access to European markets. However, the European Commission acknowledges more animals could have been used if tests are already being commissioned 'for other purposes'. This admission flags up one of the major loopholes that companies like Procter & Gamble [P&G] are likely to try to exploit.

The worry is that companies will continue to use ingredients tested on animals in cosmetics by pretending the test was for another purpose such as 'household products' or 'pharmaceutical'. This would be particularly easy for companies who produce different types of products in addition to cosmetics, such as household cleaners and pharmaceuticals. Indeed, in a leaked internal memo, P&G discuss how they can get round the EU law.

The worry is that companies will continue to use ingredients tested on animals in cosmetics by pretending the test was for another purpose.

But it's not just companies that are sticking two fingers up to the rule of law—meet the UK [United Kingdom] Government. An ongoing Uncaged investigation reveals that there are potentially serious weaknesses in the way the UK Government is implementing the EU law:

- They are deceiving MPs [members of Parliament] and the public, and blocking the release of animal testing information relating to products on sale in the UK.

- They require local councils' Trading Standards departments (TSDs) to implement the law. But TSDs aren't and can't enforce this as they don't have sufficient resources and expertise. So we have a catch-22 situation where TSDs will investigate if there is evidence of wrongdoing, but it is impossible to obtain evidence as it is deemed confidential.

Official Secrecy

Under the Cosmetic Products (Safety) Regulations 2008—the UK law which implements the EU law—cosmetics products manufacturers are obliged to collate information on animal testing in Product Information Packs (PIPs). These are to be made available to the Department for Business, Enterprise & Regulatory Reform (BERR) [currently the Department for Business, Innovation & Skills], and local TSDs.

Initially, the Government gave the impression that animal testing information could be obtained by the public. On 25 May 2008, Gareth Thomas MP, Minister for State at BERR, told Linda Gilroy MP:

Anybody who is concerned that a product or its ingredients have been tested illegally on animals should speak to their local Trading Standards department.

Again, in October [2009], [Justice] Minister Claire Ward told MPs that the PIPs:

will contain information on any animal testing that has been carried out in the past. If . . . members are contacted by constituents with concerns about such matters, they can refer them to their local Trading Standards department.

Information about animal testing can easily be edited to remove any genuine commercial secrets.

After we'd pointed out to MPs that TSDs couldn't give that information, BERR Minister Gareth Thomas MP admitted:

Although this information ["whether certain cosmetics products have at any stage been tested on animals"] may form part of the product information packages which all cosmetic suppliers must maintain and provide to Trading Standards officers when requested to do so, the information provided is commercially sensitive and is not to be passed on to anyone outside the enforcement service. Anyone who wishes to find out the animal testing policies of a particular company should contact the company direct.

Information about animal testing can easily be edited to remove any genuine commercial secrets, so the Government's decision to keep that information secret is perverse and contrary to the public interest. Moreover, as we are all well aware, Thomas's suggestion that people write to the companies is ludicrous as there is no obligation for companies to give truthful information about their animal testing and in fact companies who test on animals go out of their way to mislead consumers. Meanwhile, our survey of TSDs reveals their confusion and inability to enforce animal testing regulations.

Animal Experimentation Rates in the United Kingdom Have Dramatically Increased

Steve Connor

Steve Connor is the science editor for the Independent *from which the following viewpoint is taken. He argues that the number of animals in scientific experiments in the United Kingdom increased exponentially since 2000. More troubling, Connor asserts, is that between 2007 and 2008, the number rose by 15 percent. Scientists have explained this trend as being the result of an increase in funding of biomedical experiments. Opponents of animal testing, Connor notes, urge the government and the people of the United Kingdom to see this dramatic increase as a call for action to end these practices.*

As you read, consider the following questions:

1. By what percentage has the number of animals used in experiments in the United Kingdom increased since 1997, according to Connor?

2. By what percentage does Connor say the number of fish used in experiments in the United Kingdom increased between 2007 and 2008?

3. From 1996 to 2006, how much did the funding of biomedical research in the United Kingdom increase, according to Simon Festing?

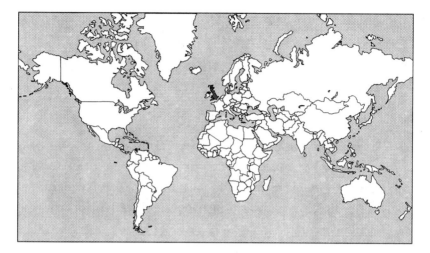

The number of animals used in scientific research last year rose by 15 per cent on the previous year bringing the total to nearly 3.6 million—the greatest number of animals involved in laboratory experiments for almost 20 years.

Statistics released today by the Home Office showed that the number of experiments involving animals that were started in 2008 also rose by about 14 per cent to just under 3.7 million "procedures", an increase that closely matched the total number of animals used. This represents a 39 per cent increase in animal experiments since Labour came to power in 1997.

[2008's] increase in the number of animal experiments was the biggest for more than two decades.

The number of animals used in experiments had begun to fall in the 1990s but in the past decade it has increased steadily each year largely due to the rise in the number of genetically modified mice used in biomedical research. Last year's increase in the number of animal experiments was the biggest for more than two decades.

Lord West, the Home Office minister responsible for regulating animal research, said that an overall increase in the amount of biomedical research carried out in Britain largely explains why there has been such a large rise in the number of animals used in experiments as well as the increase in procedures.

"Today's statistics show an increase in the number of procedures being undertaken, and the overall level of scientific procedures is determined by a number of factors, including the economic climate and global trends in scientific endeavour," Lord West said.

"As the regulator we ensure that a proper balance between animal welfare and scientific advancement is maintained, and that the regulatory system is effective, efficient and impartial," he said.

Mice, rats and other rodents accounted for the vast majority of the animals used in 2008—some 77 per cent of the total. There was a 9 per cent increase in the use of mice compared to 2007, but much of the overall increase in the number of animals was due to an 85 per cent increase in the use of fish, which rose by 278,000.

"The increased use of mice was associated with fundamental biological research, applied studies for human medicine or dentistry and breeding. But this increase was partly accounted for by a change in the stage of development at which fish fry were counted," says the Home Office report "Statistics of Scientific Procedures on Living Animals Great Britain 2008."

Other animal groups that also experienced significant increases in experimentation included amphibians, up 15,000 (a rise of 81 per cent), pigs, up 3,600 (114 per cent), sheep, up 3,100 (9 per cent), turkeys, up 1,500 (135 per cent) and ferrets, up 680 (154 per cent). The number of macaque monkeys used in research also rose by 1,050, an increase of 33 per cent on the previous year.

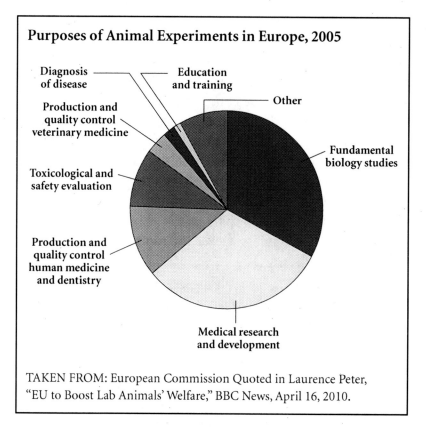

Purposes of Animal Experiments in Europe, 2005

Diagnosis of disease

Education and training

Other

Production and quality control veterinary medicine

Fundamental biology studies

Toxicological and safety evaluation

Production and quality control human medicine and dentistry

Medical research and development

TAKEN FROM: European Commission Quoted in Laurence Peter, "EU to Boost Lab Animals' Welfare," BBC News, April 16, 2010.

Animal rights groups condemned the increases on the grounds that they represent a betrayal of the avowed promise by the Government to reduce the amount of animal suffering in scientific research by a policy of replacing, reducing and refining animal experiments wherever possible.

"Such a shocking increase in animal experiments should be a wake-up call moment for policy makers that considerably more effort must be focused on the development of alternatives [to animals] in biomedical research," said Sebastien Farnaud, science director of the Dr Hadwen Trust charity.

"[This is] not simply to avoid animal suffering but crucially so that medical research can benefit from the advantages that nonanimal approaches can bring," Dr Farnaud said.

Michelle Thew, chief executive of the British Union for the Abolition of Vivisection, said: "This shocking rise in the numbers of animals subjected to experiments is an outrage. This is the seventh year of consecutive rises in the number of animals used. There is clear public concern on this issue."

However, Simon Festing, executive director of Understanding Animal Research, said that the increases show that Britain is doing more and better research to find solutions to serious diseases. "This is a continuation of the trend which saw funding of biomedical research increase in real terms by over 50 per cent in the decade to 2006, while animal procedures increased by just 12.5 per cent over the same period," he said.

"This shocking rise in the numbers of animals subjected to experiments is an outrage."

A spokesman for the Association of the British Pharmaceuticals Industry said that the increase in animal experiments was in large part down to the success of the scientific community in Britain. Due to it being recognised as among the best in the world, investment within academia and within industry is going up, he said.

"In 2006, spending on R&D was just under £4bn and by 2007 that figure had risen by 14.7 per cent to around £4.5bn. This is more than ever before. Consequently, there is a related rise in animal research, but the rate is not like-for-like—it is smaller due to all the work being carried out to reduce the need for animal research," he said.

Periodical and Internet Sources Bibliography

The following articles have been selected to supplement the diverse views presented in this chapter.

Alan Dove	"The Search for Animal Alternatives," *Drug Discovery and Development*, vol. 13, no. 4, May 2010.
Simon Festing	"Don't Waste the Animals," *New Scientist*, June 5, 2010.
Mehdi Ghasemi and Ahmad Reza Dehpour	"Ethical Considerations in Animal Studies," *Journal of Medical Ethics & History of Medicine*, vol. 2, no. 1, 2009.
Alan M. Goldberg and Thomas Hartung	"Protecting More Than Animals," *Scientific American*, December 26, 2005.
Tora Holmberg	"A Feeling for the Animal: On Becoming an Experimentalist," *Society and Animals*, vol. 16, no. 4, 2008.
Samia A. Hurst and Alex Mauron	"Articulating the Balance of Interests Between Humans and Other Animals," *American Journal of Bioethics*, vol. 9, no. 5, May 2009.
Andrew Knight	"No Animals Were Harmed in the Writing of This Article," *Irish Veterinary Journal*, vol. 62, no. 10, 2009.
Dan Matthews	"What Has the Animal Rights Movement Done for Animal Welfare?" *Biologist*, February 2010.
Viren Swami, Adrian Furnham, and Andrew N. Christopher	"Free the Animals? Investigating Attitudes Toward Animal Testing in Britain and the United States," *Scandinavian Journal of Psychology*, vol. 49, no. 3, June 2008.
Tzachi Zamir	"Killing for Knowledge," *Journal of Applied Philosophy*, vol. 23, no. 1, 2006.

 GLOBALVIEWPOINTS

CHAPTER 3

The World Food Industry and Animal Welfare

Automation Systems for Farm Animals Harm Human-Animal Relationships

Cécile Cornou

Cécile Cornou is a professor in the Department of Large Animal Sciences at the University of Copenhagen in Denmark. In the following viewpoint, Cornou argues that current automation systems used in the farming industry are limited in their usefulness because they alter the relationship between animals and their human caregivers. Cornou acknowledges that such systems can be used to monitor the well-being of the animals, but they also discourage human contact, which can lead to fear of humans when the animal is sick and needs human attention.

As you read, consider the following questions:

1. When does Cornou say automation systems were first used in animal farming?

2. What are two recommended solutions for reducing the risk of animals developing a fear of humans when automation systems are used?

3. Why does Cornou say that consumers must be considered among the ethical questions of AS?

Cécile Cornou, "Automation Systems for Farm Animals: Potential Impacts on the Human-Animal Relationship and on Animal Welfare," *Anthrozoos*, vol. 22, no. 3, September 2009, pp. 213–220, by Berg Publishers, an imprint of A&C Black Publishers Ltd. Reproduced by permission.

Abstract. This article discusses ethical issues raised by automation systems in animal farming. These systems automatically collect various kinds of information about an animal and allow the farmer to monitor it remotely. It is argued that the relationship between the farmer and the individual animal is becoming increasingly distant and impoverished. Although this may protect the animal from some negative interactions, it is less clear whether use of these systems will lead to an increase in positive interactions of the kind beneficial for animal welfare. Furthermore, the measurement of specific parameters replaces observation of the animal as a whole, which may affect the perception of the animal. As automation systems replace traditional tasks, the role of the farmer is changing drastically. This may lead to deskilling in the farmer, which in turn may affect animal welfare. The value of automation systems in increasing productivity is clear; however, this paper questions the extent to which these systems can be used to enhance animal welfare. It is argued that ethically acceptable development of automation systems for farm animals can only be achieved if these systems prove to be beneficial in respect of animal welfare.

Keywords: animal welfare, automation systems, ethics, human-animal relationship

Automation systems (AS) were first used in animal husbandry in the identification systems of the late 1960s. In the mid-1970s, the first computer-controlled feeding system was manufactured by the Dutch firm DACA. During the 1980s, integrated circuit (IC) technology permitted the miniaturization of transponders. As the size of farms increased, radio frequency identification (RFID) helped farmers to identify a single animal in a large group, decreased labor costs, and improved working conditions (Rossing 1999). Later, in the 1990s, a third generation of sensor technology began to be developed. These sensors were designed to store data on, for example, the medical history of the animal, and to monitor health and performance (Eradus and Jansen 1999). Given the increasing demand for traceability and new regulations governing group housing (e.g., the European Council Directive 2001/88/EEC), the value of AS is clear.

In this article, "AS" refers either to software systems that make direct use of this third generation of sensors (the data being collected through a sensor attached to the animal); or to systems that collect information about an individual animal wearing an identification tag (and in this way, for example, recognized at the milking parlor or feeding station); or to other systems that remotely gather data about a specific parameter. These systems collect, transfer, and analyze information about a single animal, so that the farmer is informed about the state of that animal at all times. They can replace various traditional tasks of husbandry: estrus detection, weighing, and milking can now be automatically performed by AS. Current AS answer a desire to increase productivity: by a better control of reproductive performance, by allowing individual animal health status to be monitored, by improving the economic return in facilitating the delivery of more homogeneous products, and by reducing labor costs. Although a few AS have been developed for extensive production (for animal tracking using GPS, for instance, Rutter, Beresford and Roberts [1997]), this article focuses on modern intensive animal husbandry. In developed countries, the great majority of animal production units are intensive, and it is on these farms that most AS are currently being implemented and developed.

The use of AS in new methods of production may affect the stockman, the welfare of animals, and the relationship between the stockman and the animals. The importance of the human-animal relationship (HAR) upon animal productivity and welfare has been studied for various species: for example, Hemsworth and Coleman (1998) for livestock, more recently Breuer et al. (2000) and Breuer, Hemsworth and Coleman (2003) for dairy cows, and Hemsworth et al. (1999) for pigs.

The methods for assessing this relationship have also been recently reviewed (Waiblinger et al. 2006). The fact that labor-saving technology (replacing traditional tasks of husbandry, as, for example, feeding) tends to further reduce contact time between stockpersons and animals has been mentioned (Rushen, Taylor and de Passille 1999), but the influence of these technologies upon the agents involved in animal husbandry (farmers and animals) has not yet been the object of deeper discussion.

Consumers are becoming increasingly aware, and critical, of the conditions in which farm animals are raised, especially with regard to welfare issues (Lassen, Sandoe and Forkman 2006). If consumers' views of animal welfare are to be taken into consideration, it is argued that the interest and credibility of AS will depend not only on the extent to which automation systems improve animal welfare, but, before this, on a demonstration that such systems do not themselves lead to reduced welfare. The potential value of AS in reducing labor costs and improving productivity make their development within animal farming most likely; the issue is whether it would be ethically correct to employ AS when they risk altering animal welfare for the worse.

Consumers are becoming increasingly aware, and critical, of the conditions in which farm animals are raised.

In this article, it is questioned whether the implementation of AS is beneficial for both the farmer and the animal. What impact do automation systems have on the farmer, the animal, and the relationship between the farmer and the animal? To what extent can they be employed to benefit animal welfare?

The following section discusses the impact of AS upon the HAR, and some of the potential consequences upon animal welfare. The final section discusses other impacts that AS may have upon animal welfare, farmers, and consumers.

The Impact of AS on the HAR and Their Consequences for Animal Welfare

A major potential impact of AS is an increase in distance in the farmer-animal relationship, a distance already impoverished, especially in large-scale farms. This is a result of the remote monitoring of the animals: Farmers need not observe the livestock as closely as before, since information about individuals is transmitted directly to a computer.

Suppression of some of the routine farmer-animal contacts can reduce some potential negative interactions. For instance, violence towards an animal may be threatened or committed in the process of moving the animal. AS can contribute to avoidance or reduction of this violence in that it can sort, move or weigh animals automatically (using e.g., electronic gates) without human contact, and so protect the animals. It should be stressed that the relationship between the farmer and the animal also affects the farmer, since her/his handling of animals will be carefully scrutinized by society. Therefore, it can be argued that avoidance of these potential negative interactions may give the farmer more credibility in society.

A major impact of AS is an increase in distance in the farmer-animal relationship, a distance already impoverished.

Nevertheless, AS may result in more negative than positive human-animal interactions being performed. While the opportunities for positive interactions with livestock are replaced by AS (e.g., manual feeding replaced by automatic feeders, milking replaced by milking robot), some aversive tasks resulting in stress and/or pain for the animal, such as vaccination or castration, still require human intervention.

The Fastest Milking Robot

According to Ian Tossell, UK [United Kingdom] sales manager for Lely [Industries]: "The A3 Next robot is the fastest milking robot with the fastest attachment time, which means more milkings per day and more cows per robot. On average, the cow will be in the robot for about eight minutes, of which about six minutes 15 seconds will be actual milking time with the remainder spent cleaning the teats and attaching the teat cups and then spraying the teats when the cow has finished milking. The average number of milkings a day per robot will be about 160, although the number can be as high as 180."

Beth Greenaway, "Robots Run Amok,"
Engineering and Technology, *February 20, 2010.*

Overall, interactions between the farmer and the animals—both positive and negative—tend to become scarcer. Housing systems in which AS are implemented and/or assist implementation tend to further reduce potential interactions: For example, in larger groups, AS can help give an individual animal more space in which to avoid people, so that human-animal contact becomes more difficult. Also, there is a tendency to find alternative ways to attract and manipulate the animals in current AS; for example, by using music, instead of walking among the animals, to encourage the cows to walk to the automatic milking parlor (Uetake, Hurnik and Johnson 1997).

However crucial more space is for animal welfare, a consequence of this reduction of regular human-animal contact is that the animal becomes less habituated to people. As a result, contact with humans could become more distressing, thereby increasing stress and fear of humans (Rushen, Taylor and de Passille 1999) and hence reduce animal welfare. This will be a major problem when an animal needs to be treated for disease, for example. As Hemsworth and Coleman (1998) state: "another potential problem for animals that are deprived of human contact is the fact that, if any human contact is required, perhaps in an emergency situation, this interaction will be highly fear-provoking and aversive."

To improve the HAR and hinder animals from developing a fear of humans, several authors have suggested two main solutions: 1) encouraging positive human-animal interactions, and 2) ensuring a positive attitude/behavior of the stockperson towards the animal.

In connection with dairy cows, Raussi (2003) suggests that attempts should be made to ensure that there are, on balance, more positive interactions than negative ones to discourage animals from developing a fear of humans. This author also suggests that the behavior (and indeed the mere presence) of the stockperson influences the animal's fear of humans, and points out the importance of having a person who is well trained to handle the animals. Waiblinger et al. (2006) suggest that both productivity and animal welfare can improve in systems that involve regular, intense, and long-term human-animal contact. These authors also suggest modifying the farmers' attitudes and behavior through educational initiatives to alleviate the animals' fear of humans and to promote more positive human-animal relationships. According to Rushen, Taylor and de Passille (1999), solutions for reducing animals' fear of humans are found in the stockperson's behavior. Hemsworth (2003) reports that training programs targeting attitudes and behavior of stockpeople have a direct effect on animal fear, welfare and productivity. Another solution would be to completely automate the stockperson's functions; in that way, any adverse human-animal interventions could be avoided (Hemsworth and Coleman 1998). This last option is, however, not yet realistic, since particular interventions (vaccination, castration, treatment in the case of diseases) still require human contact. Finally, Anthony (2003) is also in favor of improving the human-animal bond, which may not only benefit the animal (by reducing fear and stress) but also the farmer, whom by frequent and close contact with the animal may get more familiar with the animal's disposition, needs, and behavior, potentially resulting in better detection of the animal's welfare.

It is extremely important to reflect on the ethical issues which AS raise.

According to the level of automation, AS have the potential to allow farmers to spend physically more time among their animals, as it reduces the time spent carrying out repetitive and laborious operations. The question of how this time is best used needs to be addressed. Frost et al. (1997) review developments in the use of sensors for animal farming. These sensors provide information about animal weight, animal identity, animal behavior, physiological factors, environment factors, and body conformation and composition. They use, among other things, image analysis, electronic odor sensing, and acoustic monitoring. Is there any remaining need to look at the animal directly when all this information can be automatically collected? What should any time spent directly observing livestock be used for?

It has already been suggested that the implementation of AS may result in a growing distance in the farmer-animal relationship. To put it in perspective, the already existing distance may have been necessary in modern animal husbandry. According to Rothschild (1986), such a distance may have been, and still be necessary in raising farm animals: "Just as we have to depersonalize human opponents in wartime to kill them with indifference, so we have to create a void between ourselves and the animals on which we inflict pain and misery." Hence, more positive interactions, and more time spent among his animals, might bring the farmer closer to them. The question raised here is how would the farmer respond to more time with her/his animals, if this distance is inherent in animal farming? Also, will the implementation of AS merely facilitate and increase this void, and as a result make the farmer react in an even more distanced manner to an animal in distress? And is it at all possible for the farmer to get closer to the individual animal, especially in a context where the number of animals per stockperson is constantly increasing?

Some of the issues discussed in this section (e.g., the further impoverished human-animal relationship) seem to go beyond the ones raised by the sole implementation of AS, and refer to some extent to the level and consequences of intensive systems. A reason is that both AS and intensification have developed concomitantly: AS facilitate large scale herds, and larger scale herds demand new monitoring systems. Nevertheless, reflecting on these issues is very important if AS should not only be a vehicle for further intensification, but also a vehicle to solve some of the animal welfare issues resulting from intensification.

Other Impacts of AS on Animal Welfare, Farmers and Consumers

Potential Positive Impacts

Better monitoring of the individual animal seems a priori beneficial for animal welfare. Firstly, automated monitoring of the health status of dairy cattle (Thysen 1993; de Mol and Ouweltjes 2001) or pigs (Madsen and Andersen and Kristensen 2005) can enable earlier and better detection of diseases, which in turn allow earlier treatment and, consequently, welfare improvement. These improvements concern the individual animal and/or a group of animals. Secondly, existing AS can also allow new methods for assessing animal welfare to be implemented. For instance, automated weighing of cows inside a milking robot appears to be a reliable tool to detect lameness (Pastell et al. 2006). Thirdly, AS such as milking robots, may help make routine tasks more homogeneous, thus avoiding potential variation from one stockperson to another when they perform the tasks. Finally, the use of AS permits "management by exception." That is, they provide farmers with information that helps them to focus on specific individuals in a group. In that sense, AS may assist the development of systems perceived as more "welfare-friendly," such as group housing, by allowing each animal to still be individually monitored. The fact that group housing allows, for instance, freedom of movement may help reduce chronic discomfort and hence contribute to the welfare of the animals.

With regards to farmers, the implementation of AS seems also a priori directly beneficial to them. Improving productivity results, labor conditions, and as mentioned above, animal welfare, can increase the work satisfaction of the stockperson. These potential improvements, especially with regard to animal welfare and the conditions in which animals are raised, seem also to be in the interest of the consumers.

Potential Negative Impacts

Even though data registration is already part of animal farming, it is suggested that increasing automation may result in a growing quantification/objectification of the animal. Efforts in the production system may tend to be oriented towards the improvement of specific parameters measured by AS, without necessary contact with the individual animal. This may in turn affect the attitude, and subsequent behavior of, farmers towards their livestock.

Farmers will need to prioritize new tasks, such as maintenance and management of the sensors, to ensure that the information being collected is accurate. As a result, they may depend more and more heavily on the sensors and the overall system controlling the herd. This growing dependence of farmers on computer systems may, in turn, influence their work satisfaction and increase stress. Forester and Morrison (1994) point out that the use of "computer systems can also degrade the quality of working life through 1) deskilling of the workforce, which reduces control responsibility and job satisfaction; 2) increasing stress, depersonalization, fatigue and boredom." Thomson and Schmoldt (2001) write that it is during the interim period—that is, the lag between the implementation of software and its assimilation by those who are required to work with it—that negative impacts on human quality of life are often recognized. In the present case, this interim period may be associated with more time spent learning how the automation systems in question operate and/or controlling the sensors. This may have a negative impact upon not only the performance of the traditional work carried out but also upon work satisfaction. As a further step, it is suggested that the modification of the traditional role of the farmer and a potential deskilling of the workforce risk decreasing the need for husbandry specialists.

In response to the alarms given by AS—when information that an individual is detected sick is received via a computer—the farmer should be able to give special attention to those animals. An initial issue here is that too much reliance on the sensors may lead the farmer to overlook problems that are not detected by the sensors. Also, it should be questioned whether farmers would respond as readily or efficiently to an alarm set off by a computer as they would if they saw for themselves that the animal was in distress. This remote monitoring of the animals may risk impairing the sensitivity of farmers towards their livestock, and make them less capable of taking action to treat the individual animal. Taking no action towards an individual as the result of a lack of sensitivity might be perceived as less ethical, or worse from the societal point of view, than not treating a sick animal whose illness went undetected due to inattention or negligence. Farmers need to be aware of the risks, both of overlooking other problems and/or of taking no action when an alarm is given.

If the farmer should focus on the individual animal instead of the batch or herd, how sick should an animal be before receiving a treatment? Lassen, Sandoe and Forkman (2006) suggest that "people with a background in modern animal production will probably have a bias towards focusing on the average." Also, veterinary costs may in some cases make the farmer reluctant to provide individual treatments, especially where decisions are mainly taken at the "batch" level: where priority is given to the productivity and/or welfare of the group, rather than to the individual animal. Therefore, it can be suggested that implementation of AS should come with a change of vision of livestock. Focus needs to be more oriented towards the individual animal, instead of the group of individuals, as currently occurs.

There are various ways to reflect on the welfare of farm animals, for those who attempt to enhance it. One way is to look at production-related diseases resulting from intensification, to enquire into the reasons for an animal's distress, and to reconsider the basis of the overall system. However, most current AS aim to control sickness and dysfunctionality as soon as possible, in order to prevent outbreaks of disease and reductions in welfare within the current intensive production systems. An illustration of this is the development of an AS that, by monitoring water consumption, prevents the outbreak of diarrhea in young pigs (Madsen, Andersen and Kristensen 2005). As Settle (2000) mentions: "Farmers can now be much more remote from their animals. . . . [The] scientist and the vet between them can now show the farmer new ways to stress animals for profit without actually making them sick or dysfunctional for the farmer's purposes." By means of better and faster monitoring of production diseases, some AS can hinder welfare problems that reduce productivity, without promoting better animal welfare, as such. Too much focus on animal productivity risks reducing AS merely to a control tool that maximizes profit. In this way, animal husbandry can be seen as developing in the way that other forms of industrial production have. The main associated risk is to treat our animals, even more than we already do, as products. The reduction of the animal to a machine that is monitored by a battery of sensors will undoubtedly trigger increasingly hostile public opinion. Moreover, the fact that in 1997 the European Union recognized animals as "sentient beings" makes this evolution in our perception of animals ethically undesirable.

Conclusion

The use of AS in modern animal husbandry seems at first to be only positive for animal welfare. These systems may, for example, allow earlier and better detection of diseases, and assist the development of more "welfare-friendly" housing systems. However, it has also been argued that current AS may 1) affect perceptions of the animal, which tends to be seen merely as a product or as a combination of parameters to monitor; 2) risk modifying the farmer's role, in the sense that he/she would need to develop expertise in controlling sensors and may lose the caring skills of a stockperson; and 3) impair the already impoverished relationship between farmer and animal, which may in turn affect the sensitivity of the farmer to the animal and be detrimental to animal welfare. These three elements are closely connected, since the new perception of the animals encouraged by AS may influence farmers' relationships with their livestock, especially if their role is also affected. Therefore, it is extremely important to reflect on the ethical issues which AS raise. It must be asked whether automation systems truly benefit the animals themselves, the consumer (who now seeks traceability and is more than ever aware of farm animal welfare), and the farmers who use them.

Acknowledgements

The author gratefully acknowledges Professor Peter Sandøe and Stine B. Christiansen for their comments during the preparation of this article.

References

Anthony, R. 2003. The ethical implications of the human-animal bond on the farm. *Animal Welfare* 12: 505–512.

Breuer, K., Hemsworth, P.H., Barnett, J.L., Matthews, L.R. and Coleman, G.J. 2000. Behavioural response to humans and the productivity of commercial dairy cows. *Applied Animal Behaviour Science* 66: 273–288.

Breuer, K., Hemsworth, P.H. and Coleman, G.J. 2003. The effect of positive or negative handling on the behavioural and physiological responses of nonlactating heifers. *Applied Animal Behaviour Science* 84: 3–22.

de Mol, R.M. and Ouweltjes, W. 2001. Detection model for mastitis in cows milked in an automatic milking system. *Preventive Veterinary Medicine* 49(1–2): 71–82.

Eradus, W.J. and Jansen, M.B. 1999. Animal identification and monitoring. *Computers and Electronics in Agriculture* 24(1–2): 91–98.

Forester, T. and Morrison, P. 1994. *Computer Ethics*. Cambridge, MA: MIT Press.

Frost, A.R., Schofield, C.P., Beaulah, S.A., Mottram, T.T., Lines, J.A. and Wathes, C.M. 1997. A review of livestock monitoring and the need for integrated systems. *Computers and Electronics in Agriculture* 17(2): 139–159.

Hemsworth, P.H. 2003. Human-animal interactions in livestock production. *Applied Animal Behaviour Science* 81: 185–198.

Hemsworth, P.H. and Coleman, G.J. eds. 1998. *Human-Livestock Interactions.* CAB International, UK.

Hemsworth, P.H., Pedersen, V., Cox, M., Cronin, G.M. and Coleman, G.J. 1999. A note on the relationship between the behavioural response of lactating sows to humans and the survival of their piglets. *Applied Animal Behaviour Science* 65: 43–52.

Lassen, J., Sandoe, P. and Forkman, B. 2006. Happy pigs are dirty! - conflicting perspectives on animal welfare. *Livestock Science* 103: 221–230.

Madsen, T.N., Andersen, S. and Kristensen, A.R. 2005. Modelling the drinking patterns of young pigs using a state space model. *Computers and Electronics in Agriculture* 48: 39–61.

Pastell, M., Takko, H., Gröhn, H., Hautala, M., Poikalainen, V., Praks, J., Veermäe, I., Kujala, M. and Ahokas, J. 2006. Assessing cows' welfare: weighing the cow in a milking robot. *Biosystems Engineering* 93(1): 81–87.

Raussi, S. 2003. Human-cattle interactions in group housing. *Applied Animal Behaviour Science* 80(3): 245–262.

Rossing, W. 1999. Animal identification: introduction and history. *Computers and Electronics in Agriculture* 24(1–2): 1–4.

Rothschild, M. ed. 1986. *Animal and Man.* Oxford: Clarendon Press.

Rushen, J., Taylor, A.A. and de Passille, A.M. 1999. Domestic animals' fear of humans and its effect on their welfare. *Applied Animal Behaviour Science* 65: 285–303.

Rutter, S.M., Beresford, N.A. and Roberts, G. 1997. Use of gps to identify the grazing areas of hill sheep. *Computers and Electronics in Agriculture* 17(2): 177–188.

Settle, T. 2000. Farm animals' challenge to ecological thinking: Skepticism about the prospects for an inclusive ethics of health. *Ethics and the Environment* 5(2): 243–251.

Thomson, A.J. and Schmoldt, D.L. 2001. Ethics in computer software design and development. *Computers and Electronics in Agriculture* 30(1–3): 85–102.

Thysen, I. 1993. Monitoring bulk tank somatic cell counts by a multiprocess kalman filter. *Acta Agriculturae Scandinavica, Section A—Animal Sciences* 43: 58–64.

Uetake, K., Hurnik, J.F. and Johnson, L. 1997. Effect of music on voluntary approach of dairy cows to an automatic milking system. *Applied Animal Behaviour Science* 53(3): 175–182.

Waiblinger, S., Boivin, X., Pedersen, V., Tosi, M.V, Janczak, A.M., Visser, E.K. and Jones, R.B. 2006. Assessing the human-animal relationship in farmed species: A critical review. *Applied Animal Behaviour Science* 101: 185–242.

Farmed Fish Suffer from Poor Conditions Across the Globe

The Humane Society of the United States

The Human Society of the United States is the nation's largest animal protection agency. In the following viewpoint, the society argues that farmed fish and other aquatic creatures are in danger. Not only is the number of fish, including shellfish, rapidly decreasing as the world's human population grows, but also the conditions under which the fish are farmed are inhumane. Although some scientists assert that fish do not feel pain and do not have consciousness, other scientists insist otherwise. The authors note that fish and other aquatic creatures should be given proper consideration for their welfare.

As you read, consider the following questions:

1. By what year is the global population of wild-caught aquatic animals expected to be exhausted?
2. What are the "Five Freedoms" to fish?
3. What mortality rates do some aquaculture systems suffer, according to the viewpoint?

If fisheries sustain their current yields, populations of wild-caught aquatic animals face uncertain futures, with predictions of global collapse by 2048 of all species currently fished.

"The wild harvest of seafood, man's last major hunting and gathering activity, is at a critical point," wrote U.S. Department of Agriculture (USDA) researcher David Harvey. "Technology has enabled harvesting to outpace the speed at which species can reproduce."

Depleting the World's Waterways

According to the Population Division of the Department of Economic and Social Affairs of the United Nations Secretariat, the human population of 6.09 billion in 2000 is estimated to reach 8.2 billion by 2030. Globally, the average per-capita fish and shellfish consumption each year from 2001 to 2003 was 16.4 kg (36.2 lbs) and is predicted to increase to 22.5 kg (49.6 lbs) by 2030. Indeed, given that consumption has outpaced the growth of the world's human population since the 1960s, the world's fisheries are unlikely to satisfy the marketplace. "In response," continued Harvey, "the seafood industry is beginning to shift from wild harvest to aquaculture, the production of aquatic plants and animals under grower-controlled conditions."

Absent the additional demands placed on fish supply by the increasing human population, the Food and Agriculture Organization (FAO) of the United Nations predicted in 2006 that worldwide aquaculture production must nearly double in the next 25 years to satisfy current worldwide consumptive patterns for fish. Since the mid-1980s, the aquaculture industry has expanded approximately 8% per year, and the numbers of farmed fish are expected to continue to increase, perhaps surpassing the numbers of wild-caught animals from the world's fisheries. Tore Håstein of Norway's National Veterinary Institute addressed the World Organisation for Animal Health (OIE) Global Conference on Animal Welfare in 2004 and reported that aquaculture has "developed to become the fastest growing food production sector in the world and it will continue to grow in the years to come."

With the expansion of the fish farming industry comes growing concern for the well-being of increasing numbers of aquatic animals raised and killed for human consumption. A review of recent scientific literature on fish welfare and stress, as well as debates on pain and consciousness in fish, reflect the escalating interest in the well-being of farm-raised fish. This area of research was considered so important that both *Diseases of Aquatic Organisms* and *Applied Animal Behaviour Science* devoted entire issues to the subject of behavior and welfare of fish. Beyond the scientific community, concern for fish welfare is also receiving attention, including amongst industry. The Fisheries Society of the British Isles (FSBI) states: "In practical terms also, it is often in our selfish interest to consider the issue of animal welfare; for example . . . poor welfare of farmed fish often equates to poor production."

It is . . . critical that producers act now to develop methods to ensure the health and welfare of the increasing numbers of farmed fish.

With the expected growth of the human population and increased per-capita fish consumption, the aquaculture industry will likely continue to experience growth. It is therefore critical that producers act now to develop methods to ensure the health and welfare of the increasing numbers of farmed fish. . . .

Pain Perception and Consciousness

Despite the current body of evidence regarding the welfare of farmed fish, some arguments persist that their ability to suffer and their conscious awareness of stimuli are yet to be determined. As such, two conflicting positions exist: one that contends that fish have the mental capacity to suffer and feel pain, and another that asserts that fish brains lack a key neuroanatomical structure, the neocortex—which, in humans, is associated with the generation of conscious, subjective states—so, the animals have no consciousness or capacity to feel pain.

On reviewing the evidence for nociception, or the ability to perceive and transmit signals of noxious stimuli [the perception of pain], scientists are in agreement that fish have both the appropriate nerves and pathways to sense and send potentially painful signals and that fish share neurotransmitters responsible for pain transmission with mammals, which are found in higher concentrations in brain regions receiving input from these nerves. Håstein concludes, "It is beyond doubt that fish do have nosiceptors [sic] and thus have the possibility to register pain, although the response and way of 'showing' pain is not expressed the same way as in terrestrial animals."

Scientists are in agreement that fish have both the appropriate nerves and pathways to sense and send potentially painful signals.

Lynne U. Sneddon of the University of Liverpool's School of Biological Sciences and her co-authors believe that showing physiological and behavioral responses to painful stimuli are suggestive of the perception of pain in fish. Investigating the effects of noxious substances injected into the lips of trout, the researchers observed significant changes in physiology and behavior, including increased gill, or opercular, beat rate and time to resume feeding. Sneddon *et al.* also reported that the fish, after being injected in their lips, rubbed their mouths against the sides of the tank and the gravel, and displayed rocking behaviors for up to 90 minutes post-injection—behaviors she feels are not simple reflexes and that were mitigated by application of an analgesic. The scientists concluded: "If a noxious event has sufficiently adverse effects on behaviour and physiology in an animal and this experience is painful in humans, then it is likely to be painful in the animal."

Weighing the Evidence

Arguing against the idea that fish have the ability to suffer and feel pain, James D. Rose, a professor in the Department of Zoology and Physiology at the University of Wyoming, stresses that fish lack a neocortex, which he contends is essential for consciousness. Though he agrees that noxious stimuli can evoke neural activity leading to physiological stress and behavioral responses, and further acknowledges that nociceptive reactions are universal in the animal kingdom, Rose distinguishes this from sentience stating that "reactivity to noxious stimuli does not imply conscious awareness." His primary argument distinguishes between behavioral responses to potentially painful stimuli and conscious, painful experiences where "functions of specific regions of cerebral cortex" allow humans to be aware of pain. . . .

John Webster, University of Bristol emeritus professor of animal husbandry and founding member of the Farm Animal Welfare Council, an independent advisory body established by the British government in 1979 "to keep under review the welfare of farm animals on agricultural land, at market, in transit and at the place of slaughter; and to advise the Government of any legislative or other changes that may be necessary," synthesized the discussion in a 2005 interview with the *Daily Telegraph*: "A powerful portfolio of physiological and behavioural evidence now exists to support the case that fish feel pain and that this feeling matters. In the face of such evidence, any argument to the contrary based on the claim that fish 'do not have the right sort of brain' can no longer be called scientific. It is just obstinate."

The Welfare of Aquaculture Animals

Given the myriad and fundamental differences between farmed fish and other animals raised for human consumption, it follows that welfare considerations common to land-based farmed animals may not be directly applicable to aquatic

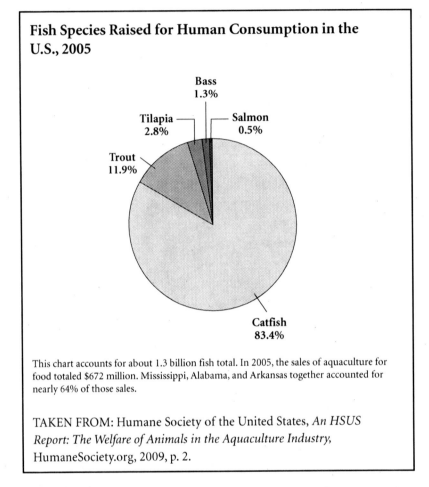

Fish Species Raised for Human Consumption in the U.S., 2005

Bass 1.3%

Tilapia 2.8%

Salmon 0.5%

Trout 11.9%

Catfish 83.4%

This chart accounts for about 1.3 billion fish total. In 2005, the sales of aquaculture for food totaled $672 million. Mississippi, Alabama, and Arkansas together accounted for nearly 64% of those sales.

TAKEN FROM: Humane Society of the United States, *An HSUS Report: The Welfare of Animals in the Aquaculture Industry,* HumaneSociety.org, 2009, p. 2.

farmed animals. Contributing greater complexity to the farmed fish welfare discussion are the challenges of separating the different effects of individual production factors, leading to, as [Professor Felicity] Huntingford *et al.* put it, "the important conclusion that, even for a particular species, gender and age of fish, we cannot guarantee the welfare by defining a simple set of husbandry conditions. This in turn emphasizes the need for sensitive on-the-spot indicators of welfare."

The FSBI [Fisheries Society for the British Isles], the "premier society in the British Isles, and increasingly in Europe, catering for the interests of professional fish biologists and fisheries managers" and publisher of the *Journal of Fish Biology*, identifies several directly observable indices of welfare, including:

- changes in skin or eye color, often indicating exposure to adverse events;

- changes in ventilation rate observed as increased opercular beating, indicating stress or exposure to environmental contaminants;

- changes in swimming performance and other behaviors, indicating injuries, the presence of parasites, or generally decreased welfare;

- reduced food intake, often indicating acute or chronic stress;

- loss of body condition or impaired growth, indicating possible chronic stress;

- morphological abnormalities resulting from the effects of adverse conditions on development;

- occurrence of injuries from aggression and slow healing, indicating possible poor immune response; and

- increased incidence of disease, indicating possible poor environmental conditions.

To align welfare issues with those commonly considered for land animals, several scientists have adapted the [UK government's] Brambell Committee's "Five Freedoms" to fish, summarized as follows:

1. Freedom from hunger and thirst: Captive fish should have a nutritionally appropriate diet to avoid decreased welfare; smolting fish may become dehydrated if transferred to sea water at too young of an age, before they are able to survive.

2. Freedom from discomfort: Appropriate water conditions should be provided as fish, through the surface area of their gills, are in intimate contact with their environment. Factors to be considered include levels of dissolved oxygen, pH, and ammonia; temperature; flow rates; and the presence of pollutants.

3. Freedom from pain, injury, and disease: While many diseases of fish may be poorly understood, they are frequently caused by problems with the environment. When outbreaks occur, they can lead to high mortality rates. All attempts should be made to limit disease outbreaks, and when disease is found, it should be quickly diagnosed and treated.

4. Freedom to express normal behavior: Appropriate densities and environmental conditions to enable the fish to exhibit natural behaviors should be maintained throughout the life cycle.

5. Freedom from fear and distress: Factors that cause fear, distress, discomfort, and other welfare-impairing conditions should be minimized.

Welfare considerations common to land-based farmed animals may not be directly applicable to aquatic farmed animals.

Fish reared in aquaculture systems face numerous welfare challenges. The development, implementation, and management of appropriate production practices and facilities to ensure the well-being of growing numbers of farmed fish are critical, as significant concerns with stress responses, water and environmental quality, stocking densities, disease and parasites, selective breeding, genetic selection and transgenic manipulation, nutrition and feed, external impacts, crowding, handling, netting and grading, transport, and stunning and slaughter contribute to decreased welfare. . . .

The Welfare of Fish Is Ignored

According to the FSBI, "[t]he scientific study of fish welfare lags behind that of the welfare of other vertebrates." At a global animal welfare conference, Håstein identified the "need to critically review all aspects and procedures in modern fish farming in order to establish ethically acceptable farming conditions, feeding and handling regimes, transport, stunning and slaughter methods." Given the billions of fish farmed domestically and globally, the need to understand the implications of aquaculture practices on those animals is critical. Indeed even despite his contention that fish are not sentient—a position highly disputed by the scientific community—Rose concludes that this "in no way devalues fishes or diminishes our responsibility for respectful and responsible stewardship of them."

All aspects of aquaculture production should be evaluated to minimize the stress and welfare assaults that fish face.

According to Håstein *et al.*, "[a]pplying the principles of ethics and animal welfare to poikilothermic aquatic animals involves supplying the things necessary for sustaining life, optimising health and minimising visible discomfort (e.g., pain, stress and fear)." The experience of multiple stressors present at every stage of aquaculture production substantially increases the stress response in fish, which, in turn, affects aspects of physiology, response to predators, and mortality as [researcher] Pickering warns, "chronic mortalities occur and, to a large extent, reflect the levels of stress to which the fish are subjected." Increasing mortalities are a clear indication that serious welfare problems exist, often from environmental effects, poor water quality, and infections, with some systems maintaining mortality rates of nearly 30% throughout the life cycle.

All aspects of aquaculture production should be evaluated to minimize the stress and welfare assaults that fish face. These animals should be afforded the proper environment, water quality, and space to enable them the full range of their natural behaviors, and be protected from stress, disease, predation, negative effects of genetic selection, and inhumane slaughter.

Stressful Living Conditions for Turkeys Can Increase the Rates of Foodborne Illness in the United States

Agricultural Research Service

In the following viewpoint, Agricultural Research Service (ARS), the in-house research arm of the US Department of Agriculture, hypothesizes that stress factors increase the number of pathogens in turkeys and that understanding how the turkey immune system is affected by stress will help the development of ways to improve turkey health. ARS discusses the effects of fatty acids on foodborne pathogens, of transport stress on turkeys, of ascorbic acid on bacterial colonization, of yeast extract on modulating bacteria-killing cells, of environmental exposure to E. coli on infection by the Listeria *pathogen, and of suppression of the immune system by dexamethasone, as well as using the output of avian antimicrobial peptides to measure the effectiveness of immune system enhancing agents.*

As you read, consider the following questions:

1. According to Agricultural Research Service, are slow-growing or fast-growing turkeys stressed more by transport? What problem did these stressed turkeys develop?

Agricultural Research Service, "Investigating the Impact of Stress on Foodborne Pathogen Colonization in Turkeys," *2009 Annual Report*, United States Department of Agriculture, January 10, 2011.

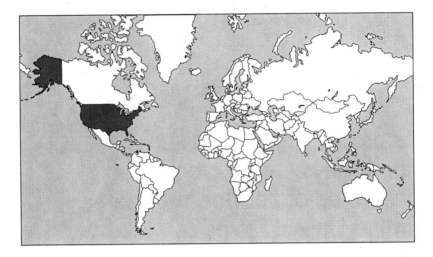

2. What complications can develop in turkeys with the use of yeast extract to boost the immune response?

3. What two conditions can increase the colonization of joint tissues of turkeys by the food pathogen *Listeria monocytogenes*?

1a. Objectives

The objectives of this work include: 1) Determine the impact of stress on the immune response and on colonization of foodborne pathogens in turkeys; 2) Optimize strategies for decreasing the impact of stress on colonization of turkeys with pathogens of food safety importance.

1b. Approach

We hypothesize that the response to common stressors of commercial turkey production, including *Escherichia coli [E. coli]* respiratory disease (airsacculitis), moving and transport, and temperature extremes, can increase pre-harvest contamination of turkeys with pathogens of food safety importance, and that basic understanding of how turkey immunity is affected by stress will lead to the development and application of practical strategies to improve product safety. Because stress has been shown to both increase disease resistance at low levels and decrease disease resistance at high or sustained levels, its effects on food safety have been difficult to quantify. We have developed transport stress and cold stress models which result in repeatable levels of stress-induced infection of turkeys with *E. coli*. We will use these models to study the colonization of turkeys with other bacteria of food safety importance. Cell culture studies of the interaction between bacterial pathogens and primary turkey synovial cells, macrophages, and heterophils [cells that fight infection], from normal and stressed animals, will provide basic data and systems for testing the efficacy of therapeutic and prophylactic [preventive] products to modulate the stress response, improve disease resistance, and decrease carcass contamination with pathogens. Novel nonantibiotic interventions will include antimicrobial peptides [compounds formed from parts of amino acids] and acute phase proteins that will be developed using exploratory analysis of physiological reactions in our stress models as described in the previous section. These products will be incorporated into stress models; however, variations in both dosage and timing relative to stressor will be emphasized in multiple experiments to maximize production gains while minimizing pathogen contamination.

Modern commercial turkey lines may become increasingly susceptible to stress-induced immunosuppression and resulting opportunistic bacterial infections as selection continues for fast growth.

---

3. Progress Report

Progress has been made toward the development of immune assays for measuring heterophil responses to stress and infection. We have documented the deleterious effects of transporting fast-growing turkeys to larger facilities on physiology, immunity, and production values. We have determined that ascorbic acid has differential effects on slow-growing and fast-growing turkeys.

4. Accomplishments

1. Feeding natural fatty acids reduces foodborne pathogens in poultry: *Campylobacter* and *Salmonella* cause human foodborne illness, and epidemiological evidence indicates poultry and poultry products as a significant source of human infection. Reducing these pathogens in poultry would reduce contamination of food products. Collaborative studies by scientists in the Poultry Production and Product Safety Research Unit with the University of Arkansas and the University of Connecticut demonstrated prophylactic and therapeutic efficacy of feed-supplemented fatty acid, caprylic acid, against *Campylobacter* and *Salmonella* in poultry. Antibiotic alternatives to reducing these pathogens are an important strategy to improving food safety of poultry production in the US.

2. Fast-growing turkeys more susceptible to transport stress: Scientist in the Poultry Production and Product Safety Research Unit determined that transport stress and *Escherichia coli* challenge were more deleterious [harmful] in a line of turkeys genetically selected for increased 16-week body weight when compared to its slow-growing parent line. This suggests that modern commercial turkey lines may become increasingly susceptible to stress-induced immunosuppression [suppression or weakening of the immune system that defends the body against illness] and resulting opportunistic bacterial infections as selection continues for fast growth. The transport stress model mimicked the commercial practice of moving poults from the brooder house to a larger grow-out house at 5 weeks of age. The fast-growing turkeys that were transported and challenged were unable to eliminate *E. coli* from both the air sac and liver at 3 days post-challenge. Alternative manage-

ment systems that allow poults to remain in the same facility throughout production may improve turkey health and the safety of turkey products.

3. Ascorbic acid may increase bacterial colonization in fast-growing turkeys: Ascorbic acid (Vitamin C) has previously shown both good and bad effects in stress and disease models. Scientists in the Poultry Production and Product Safety Research Unit determined that a 24-hour ascorbic acid treatment prior to transport stress was able to modulate the levels of stress hormone (corticosterone) in a slow-growing parent line of turkeys, but not in turkeys selected for fast growth. Ascorbic acid decreased the heterophil/lymphocyte ratio, which is a way to measure stress in birds, in the fast-growing line but not in the parent line, and this decrease was associated with a failure to clear *E. coli* from the air sac 3 days post-challenge. This research provides evidence of the need for caution when supplementing fast-growing poultry with ascorbic acid.

Dexamethasone immunosuppression . . . results in cellulitis lesions characteristic of the emerging disease clostridial dermatitis of turkeys. This disease results in high levels of mortality of production-age birds.

---

4. Yeast extract modulates bacteria-killing cells in transport stressed turkeys: Yeast extracts contain biological response modifiers that may be useful as alternatives to antibiotics for controlling pathogens in poultry production and preventing the negative effects of production stressors. Scientists in the Poultry Production and Product Safety Research Unit discovered that a yeast extract feed supplement (Alphamune) was able to increase the percentages of bacteria-killing cells and the ability of these cells to kill bacteria, and these changes were correlated with a decrease in the isolation of *E. coli* from both air sacs and livers of birds fed the supplemented diet. In

addition, yeast extract modulated the dramatic increase in activity of bacteria-killing cells due to transport stress. While activation is an important component of the innate immune response, the bacteria-killing cells are also responsible for inflammatory tissue damage. This study suggests that yeast extract supplementation may help to modulate the stress response in turkeys challenged with *E. coli* and subjected to transport stress.

5. Environmental exposure to *E. coli* can increase colonization of turkeys with the food pathogen *Listeria monocytogenes*: Scientists in the Poultry Production and Product Safety Research Unit have found that concurrent environmental exposure to an *Escherichia coli* challenge increased *L. monocytogenes* colonization of joint tissues in birds that were immunosuppressed with dexamethasone. Transport stress of challenged birds decreased *L. monocytogenes* colonization of joint tissues in the same study. This emphasizes the bi-phasic [having two phases] nature of the stress response, in that severe stress can be immunosuppressive while moderate stress can be beneficial. These results suggest that environmentally acquired *L. monocytogenes* can transiently colonize the joint tissues of severely stressed turkeys and may be a sporadic source of contamination of processing plants with a persistent type of *L. monocytogenes*.

6. Dexamethasone immunosuppression results in high incidence of dermatitis [inflammation of the skin]: Scientists in the Poultry Production and Product Safety Research Unit documented that a dexamethasone (Dex) model for stress-induced immunosuppression results in cellulitis lesions characteristic of the emerging disease clostridial dermatitis of turkeys. This disease results in high levels of mortality of production-age birds. The high incidence of dermatitis in Dex-treated birds (33-72%) and the prevalence of this production problem in male turkeys nearing market age, suggests

that production stress is involved in the etiology and that a stress challenge model may be useful for development of preventative treatment.

7. Quantitative method for measuring avian defensins: Defensins are known to be antimicrobial peptides, but all of their physiological actions are not known. Thus, they have great potential for use in food safety, protecting against microbial agents. To realize this potential, they need to be understood better. Scientists at the Poultry Production and Product Safety Research Unit in Fayetteville, Arkansas, characterized bacterial-killing peptides that were isolates from chicken and turkey blood cells. Using these peptides, called avian beta defensins-2 (AvBD2), similar peptides were identified in pheasant and quail, purified from bone marrow of the respective species, and sequenced using mass spectrometry. Using chemical modification and mass spectrometry, a method was developed to determine the amount of these peptides following stimulation of blood cells with different immunomodulating agents. Besides defensins being produced by heterophils, the cells that fight infection, they can be useful as biomarkers of stress and disease.

Polish Factory Farms Are Hazardous to the Well-Being of Pigs

Jo Knowsley and Richard Sadler

Jo Knowsley and Richard Sadler are journalists who contribute to the Mail on Sunday *and to the* Independent on Sunday. *They report on an investigation of the conditions of factory farms in Poland by the campaign group Compassion in World Farming. A large percentage of pork processed in Poland is exported to the United Kingdom. Knowsley and Sadler also report that tracking down the origin of pork sold in retail outlets in the United Kingdom is difficult. Liberal labeling laws make it nearly impossible for consumers to tell the country of origin of their meat products.*

As you read, consider the following questions:

1. What percentage of pork on sale in Britain do Knowsley and Sadler claim is produced in Britain?

2. How many tonnes of pork products does the UK import, according to the viewpoint? How many tons come from Poland?

3. There are at least three buyers and sellers of pork products in the UK mentioned by the authors. Who are they, and what is said about the pork that they sell?

In another incident, a pig in a slaughterhouse in Hungary is seen being hit over the head with an axe handle, a form of stunning that is illegal.

Since CIWF launched its investigation, Polish authorities have announced that the slaughtermen on film will be prosecuted. And they are working to bring laws into line with western Europe.

British imports of pork and products such as bacon increased by 14 per cent last year to nearly 770,000 tonnes.

Mick Sloyan, of the British Pig Executive, said: 'We believe that some 70 per cent of these imports came from pigs raised in conditions that would not conform to United Kingdom minimum legal standards.' Nearly 70 per cent of fresh pork sold in the UK is British, while almost all of the fresh pork sold by Marks & Spencer and Waitrose is British.

But only 23 per cent of bacon and ten per cent of ham sold here is British, as shown by the Quality Standard Mark.

Safeway said it did not sell fresh pork from Poland but did stock some specialist Polish hams. A spokesman said: 'We can't comment on ready-meals that are not our own brand.' Sainsbury's stocks of fresh pork are all British, but it sells Polish sausages 'from approved factories and authentically sourced'.

Tesco said none of its pork came from Poland but it could not guarantee the meat was not in ready-meals that were not its own brand.

It is, of course, impossible for the supermarkets to know which of their suppliers, if any, are using meat from the dubious abattoirs.

But campaigners hope that moves to improve labelling and animal welfare in the new EU countries will end any chance that the meat we consume has been inhumanely slaughtered.

Periodical and Internet Sources Bibliography

The following articles have been selected to supplement the diverse views presented in this chapter.

Elizabeth Allison	"Would a Better Understanding Deter Meat-Eaters?" *Leicester Mercury* (UK), July 28, 2010.
John L. Barnet and Paul H. Hemsworth	"Welfare Monitoring Schemes: Using Research to Safeguard Welfare of Animals on the Farm," *Journal of Applied Animal Welfare Science*, vol. 12, no. 2, April 2009.
Gerry Boland	"Barbaric Cattle Boats," *Daily Mail*, August 2, 2010.
Katie Engelhart and Nicholas Köhler	"Save the Planet—Stop Eating Meat," *Maclean's*, March 30, 2010.
Martin Hickman	"New Battle of Britain as Plans for Factory Farm Revolution Looms," *Independent* (London), June 25, 2010.
Jaana Husu-Kallio	"Animal Health and Animal Welfare: Is It the Same Thing?" *Acta Veterinaria Scandinavica*, vol. 50, August 19, 2008.
F. Bailey Norwood and Jayson L. Lusk	"The Farm Animal Welfare Debate," *Choices: The Magazine of Food, Farm and Resource Issues*, vol. 24, no. 3, 2009.
Jonathan Silk	"Spare a Thought for Animals Bred for Food," *Western Morning News* (UK), August 2, 2010.
Jacqueline Tawse	"Consumer Attitudes Towards Farm Animals and Their Welfare: A Pig Production Case Study," *Bioscience Horizons*, vol. 3, no. 2, June 2010.
Bryan Walsh	"America's Food Crisis and How to Fix It," *Time*, August 20, 2009.

CHAPTER 4

Animal Ownership and Animal Welfare Around the World

International Zoos and Aquariums Can Help Save Animal Species from Extinction

A.G. Clarke

The Frozen Ark Project is a consortium of many organizations across the globe developed to collect the genetic material of threatened animal species before they become extinct. In the following viewpoint A.G. Clarke, the director of the project, argues that zoos and aquariums can play a major role in the collection of this genetic material because these institutions have access to animals. Genetic material is collected and then frozen by the project. It is hoped that at some point in the future, humans will be able to regenerate these species so that these animals can continue to live.

As you read, consider the following questions:

1. About how many species of animals have been described, in the author's estimation?
2. What four groups does the Frozen Ark Consortium bring together?
3. According to Clarke, what are some ways samples from species are collected?

A.G. Clarke, "The Frozen Ark Project: The Role of Zoos and Aquariums in Preserving the Genetic Material of Threatened Animals," *International Zoo Yearbook*, vol. 43, no. 1, 2009, pp. 222–230. Copyright © 2009 by John Wiley & Sons, Inc. Reproduced by permission.

The earth currently suffers from a bout of animal extinctions. The Frozen Ark Project is acting internationally in preserving the genetic resources of threatened wild species before they become extinct. Modern techniques make preservation of this material easier, and costs of sequencing genomes have declined drastically during the past 10 years. The project is vital because the extinction of a species results in the loss of not only the animal but also the genetic information accumulated over millions of years of evolution. It will give us the ability to invigorate conservation-breeding programmes and conserve material of practical value in the form of tissues, viable somatic cells, gametes, eggs and embryos. The Frozen Ark is not considered a substitute for saving the animals themselves but an essential 'back-up' to this activity. International collaboration between the world's zoos, aquariums, museums and universities is developing to achieve this conservation effort of last resort. Zoos and aquariums are crucial to the project because they increasingly hold the last individuals of the most threatened species.

Key-words: biobanks; captive breeding; climate change; conservation breeding; cryobanks; cryopreservation; extinction; threatened animals.

Introduction

The object of the Frozen Ark Project is to save the genetic material of threatened animal species and, where possible, their viable cells before they become extinct. In the 1980s and 1990s, several groups of people advocated the collection of frozen tissues and cells (e.g., Benirschke, 1984; Benford, 1992; Holt *et al.*, 1996). One of the first frozen storage facilities for threatened species was established in 1995 at the Animal Gene Storage and Resource Centre of Australia (AGSRCA) at the Monash Stem Cell Laboratories. Tissue samples and cell lines of native and exotic species are held and research into assisted reproduction programmes has been initiated using stored samples from a range of Australian native species.

Despite some exceptions, many tissue collections were not in a form suitable for the long-term preservation of undamaged DNA. Of those that were storing cells, most were not aimed specifically at threatened species. Little global collaboration between the institutes involved had developed and virtually nothing was being done to preserve the DNA or the viable cells of threatened invertebrates.

Plants were faring better. Kew Gardens in the United Kingdom and other institutions such as the Missouri Botanical Garden in the United States had set out to conserve viable seeds of the world's threatened plants for horticultural, agricultural and scientific purposes. The Millennium Seed Bank at Kew includes seeds from thousands of threatened plants as an insurance against the loss of the species in their natural environment, and as a research tool for scientific knowledge and for conservation (Linington, 2000).

In 2000, there was an appeal for a coordinated world effort to bank DNA and cells from threatened animals to create an international database recording where and what collections were held, and to develop cooperation between institutions holding samples (Ryder *et al.*, 2000). In 2004, the Frozen Ark Project was launched to create this database, to develop international links between institutions, to hold samples and to carry out research into the best ways of collecting and storing these materials (see http://www.frozenark.org). About two million species of animals have so far been described of the five to ten million thought to exist (May, 1988). Current rates of extinction are estimated to be 100 times higher than the typical rates found in the fossil record and it is predicted that extinction rates will increase to 1000–10000 times the background over the coming decades (Millennium Ecosystem Assessment, 2005). Species are believed to be dying out at a rate matched only in the last 300 million years of Earth's history by its three greatest extinction events, at the ends of the Permian, Triassic and Cretaceous periods. The current extinctions are largely the result of human proliferation and interference, and the destruction of the world's ecosystems, a situation increasingly exacerbated by climate change (Thomas *et al.*, 2004). WWF and the United Nations both predict that by 2070 only a few endemic animals of limited range will remain in the wild.

By 2070 only a few endemic animals of limited range will remain in the wild.

The latest International Union for Conservation of Nature (IUCN) Red Data Lists of threatened species give the current numbers of threatened animals in each category of threat (IUCN, 2007). Their figures are generally thought to be serious underestimates as fewer than 10% of the world's described species have had their conservation status determined (May, 1988; IUCN, 2007). Of those that have, over 16,000 species are identified as threatened. Among the vertebrate groups assessed, 30–50% of amphibians, 23% of mammals and 12% of birds are considered at risk (IUCN, 2007). It is believed that 75% of the world's fish stocks are fully exploited or overexploited (UNEP, 2008).

Despite growing numbers of successful conservation efforts to save individual species, it is likely that only a small percentage of all threatened species will be able to be conserved by such programmes, which can be expensive and difficult. 'Back-up' strategies for these programmes are needed urgently.

STORAGE AND USES OF GENETIC RESOURCES

DNA

Saving DNA in a form suitable for sequencing provides information that specifies the construction, organization, biochemistry, metabolism and physiology of an animal. For this, a small piece of tissue, a sample of blood or gametes need to be frozen and stored at −70 °C or, even better, at the temperature of liquid nitrogen (−196 °C). Such a preservation is now relatively cheap at around US$600 or less per species. It has been calculated that ten million samples could be stored in the volume of an average house. Knowledge of the great stability of DNA (Lindahl, 1993; Hoss *et al.*, 1996) and observations on 30 000 year-old tissues preserved in the permafrost (Poinar *et al.*, 2006) indicate that DNA kept at −70 °C or −196 °C would remain substantially intact for many thousands of years.

Apart from freezing, there are several other possible methods for the long-term storage of DNA in tissues: preservation in pure ethanol or freeze drying (reviewed by Dessauer *et al.*, 1996), as dry smears on FTA Whatman papers (Smith & Burgoyne, 2001) or with the preservative RNA*later* (Vink *et al.*, 2005). Methods that do not involve freezing may be particularly useful for storage in countries with unreliable supplies of electricity, although their suitability for the very long term needs further investigation. This topic comprises one of the tasks of the Frozen Ark research laboratory. Preliminary observations suggest that freeze-dried material stored at −20 °C, perhaps even when kept at room temperature, retains DNA in good condition for more than 30 years (D. O'Foighil & C. Wade, unpubl. data).

The cost of sequencing a whole genome (the size of a human's) has declined drastically during the last 10 years, from billions of dollars to tens of thousands, and it is predicted to decline to one thousand very shortly (Service, 2006).

The value of conserved DNA is manifold. For example, the sequence of a single gene can show the relationship of an animal with others and suggest whether it is a different species. A comparison with its closest relatives using array technology (Stoughton, 2005; Kammenga *et al.*, 2007) can highlight genetic factors related to its threatened status and can provide clues on how to ameliorate those factors. Knowledge of DNA informs us about an animal's ecological needs through its proteins. A complete DNA sequence allows any protein in the animal to be made *in vitro*. Its properties can then be investigated (e.g., temperature stability or susceptibility to environmental toxins). Many proteins studied in this way will inevitably be of veterinary, conservation or medical importance.

It is within the realms of reasonable speculation that the fast progress of molecular biology will allow us, in the not-too-distant future, to construct artificial chromosomes from known genome sequences, insert them into 'generic eggs' and produce animals that have become extinct. In the absence of suitable habitats, they could be kept in zoos and aquariums until habitats have been restored or reconstructed. In the extreme, it is our belief that it is far better to have animal species in artificial surroundings than not at all.

Viable Cells

Cell cultures of many types of somatic cells from many taxa can now be preserved and remain viable for many years at -196 °C; for example, the fibroblast cell line from the Bluegill sunfish *Lepomis macrochirus* (Zhang & Rawson, 2002). Similarly, sperm, oocytes and embryos of many animals can be cryopreserved but eggs are more susceptible to damage by freezing. In a few cases, for example in the Zebrafish *Danio reno* (Guan *et al.*, 2008) and the fruit fly *Drosophila* (Mazur *et al.*, 1992), viable frozen eggs can be produced but with difficulty. Recent observations (P. Bartels & W. Holt, unpubl. data) suggest that small lumps of mammalian tissue frozen at -196 °C can give rise to viable cell cultures. This means that sources of viable cells may be able to be stored at a cost similar to those quoted for DNA preservation alone (US$600 per species). More research is required in this area.

Stored somatic cells can provide information not only about the DNA of an animal but also about the RNA molecules and proteins that can be extracted from cultured cells.

Nuclear transfer from somatic cells allows the duplication of specific genotypes that can be used to promote the rescue of threatened captive-bred animals too inbred to survive (Wells *et al.*, 1998). Techniques are being developed that allow cells to be inserted into embryos of another species closely related to the donor. Inserted cells can then be made to differentiate into germ line cells, so that recipient species can produce donor germ cells. Crosses between ♂♂ and ♀♀ of a species that are both modified could, in principle, be used to re-create extinct species. Such techniques are discussed by Lee (2001).

Transferred sheep embryos have been shown to be viable after long-term cryopreservation (Fogarty *et al.*, 2000). Genetic resources taken from testes, epididymis and ovaries have produced viable offspring (Dresser *et al.*, 1988; Gomez *et al.*, 2007). Cultured cell lines derived from many different types of cells can potentially be used for nuclear transfer or cloning (Ryder & Benirschke, 1997; Wilmut *et al.*, 1997). The preservation of somatic cells may become an option preferable to the often difficult procedure of collecting and preserving gametes. Recent advances in cryobiology (Chao *et al.*, 1996; Crowe & Crowe, 2000) suggest that in the future small tissue or blood samples from live animals, subsequently cultured and frozen, may be the best way of acquiring genetic material. Somatic cells, once frozen and stored, can be re-cultured to provide an indefinitely renewable source of cells.

There are many technologies developed from the study of humans, livestock and laboratory animals that are emerging to help maintain genetic diversity in threatened species. These technologies will lead to management strategies for threatened species (Pukazhenthi *et al.*, 2006). Sperm stem cell transplantation within and between species has enabled the reproductive capacities of valuable animals to be preserved (Dobrinski & Travis, 2007). Cross-species nuclear transfer using post mortem somatic cells has led to the rescue of a threatened species: the European mouflon *Ovis orientalis musimon* (Loi *et al.*, 2001). The potential for somatic cell nuclear transfer to provide a unique alternative for the preservation of threatened animals has been discussed by Mastromonaco & Allan King (2007). Stored viable sperm, used in artificial insemination and other reproductive technologies, can help conservationists to re-invigorate threatened species by countering the effects of recessive deleterious genes that accumulate in small populations (Holt, 2008). The uses of modern reproductive biotechnologies, involving artificial insemination, embryo transfer, *in vitro* fertilization, gamete/embryo manipulation, semen sexing, genome resource banking and somatic cell nuclear transfer (cloning), in conservation programmes for threatened mammalian species have been reviewed by Andrabi & Maxwell (2007).

THE ORGANIZATION OF THE FROZEN ARK

The Charity

The Frozen Ark Project has been set up as a registered charity and is based at the School of Biology at the University of Nottingham in the United Kingdom. The charity office runs the charity, provides regular updates on developments and activities within the membership, is involved with the everyday affairs of the organization and the recruitment of trustees, advisory group and consortium members. It is also responsible for the development of the web site and database, the promotion of the formation of the Taxon Expert Groups and the running of regular meetings.

DNA Laboratory

The laboratory, also located at Nottingham, is holding samples, carrying out research and developing protocols for the necessary procedures. This laboratory, along with those at the Institute of Zoology (IoZ) and the Natural History Museum

(NHM) in London, lend basic equipment and provide consumables for those wishing to collect samples for the project (see the Collectors Section at http://www.frozenark.org). The centre for fundraising is also located at Nottingham. When funds allow, we plan to offer start-up grants to institutions, particularly those in the developing world needing funds to establish their own repositories.

The University is currently building a purpose-built unit for the Frozen Ark within the School of Biology, which should be completed by January 2009 and will coincide with the arrival of its first director. The building works include offices and a new research laboratory.

At the time of writing the charity has eight trustees and an advisory board of ten, drawn from universities, zoos and museums. The advisory board meets three or four times a year with the support of the NHM. The trustees meet twice a year at the University of Nottingham.

Over the last two years, connections have been developed with the wider zoo community, with talks being given at the Australasian Regional Association of Zoological Parks and Aquaria (ARAZPA) annual conference in Perth, Australia (Clarke, 2006), and at the World Association of Zoos and Aquariums (WAZA) annual meeting in Budapest (Clarke, 2007; Clarke & Rawson, 2007). This year, the Frozen Ark has become an affiliated member of WAZA.

Zoos and aquariums increasingly provide the last refuge for the most threatened groups of animals around the world.

The Consortium

The creation of the Frozen Ark Consortium brings together four diverse but essential groups of people from zoos, aquariums, museums and universities from around the world. Although they have not traditionally worked closely together, all are essential to the success of this project. Zoos and aquariums increasingly provide the last refuge for the most threatened groups of animals around the world. They have the veterinarians and staff necessary to collect cells and tissues. The museums have the capacity to store the material for the longest term (Corthals & DeSalle, 2005) and the taxonomists to identify the animals. Most molecular biologists and conservation geneticists are located in the biological departments of universities. The former have the skills to carry out the research necessary to find the best methods of sample collection, methods of preservation and storage for each of the different animal groups. The latter have the knowledge and skills to collect samples successfully in the wild.

In the United Kingdom, Nottingham University, the NHM and IoZ were the founding members of the consortium. The Institute of Applied Natural Sciences (LIRANS) at the University of Bedfordshire, the North of England Zoological Society at Chester and the East Midlands Zoological Society at Tywcross followed. In the United States, the Ambrose Monell laboratory at the American Museum of Natural History in New York and the Conservation and Research for Endangered Species laboratory at San Diego Zoo became the first international members. They were joined from Australia by AGSRCA in Melbourne and the Reproductive Biology Unit at Perth Zoo, from India by the Centre for Cellular and Molecular Biology in Hyderabad and from South Africa by the Endangered Wildlife Trust of the National Zoo in Pretoria. New Zealand joined last year with the Centre for Conservation Medicine at Auckland Zoo. Leibniz Institute for Zoo and Wildlife Research, Berlin, joined this year. Agreements are now being developed with institutions in Sri Lanka and Thailand, and there have been enquiries from Argentina, France, Spain, Brazil, Singapore, China, Taiwan and the Philippines. We believe that consortium members should be encouraged to set up their own Frozen Ark collections in their own countries. Local specialists have the best understanding of their native animals, of which species are most in need of sampling and of the best ways to go about collecting and storing material in their own region. In this way, difficulties about the ownership of genetic resources are minimized, as are many of the problems and costs of transferring samples between countries.

The majority of consortium members have drawn up Memoranda of Understanding with the Frozen Ark: mutually acceptable documents, setting out the responsibilities and activities of both parties. The Frozen Ark team in Nottingham agrees to run the charity, laboratory and database, and to act as first port of call for the collection and storage of samples in the United Kingdom. The charity office acts as the centre for communication and for the spread of information between members.

Consortium members are asked to collect and preserve samples of threatened animals in ways that cause minimal degradation of DNA and loss of cell viability. We also ask that details of samples held for the Frozen Ark should be recorded and sent to the Nottingham office for inclusion in the database. A duplicate collection of samples should be deposited in another Frozen Ark repository to minimize irreversible losses and mishaps. Members should also be willing to receive duplicate samples from elsewhere. We ask that institutions setting up their own Frozen Ark collection should label these samples specifically as part of the Frozen Ark and agree to keep them in the best possible condition for preservation in the very long term. Finally, if collections can no longer adequately be maintained, consortium members are asked to make arrangements for their transfer to another suitable facility.

The Taxon Expert Groups

Groups are being set up to look after the species of animals in each of the major phyla. To compile these lists the IUCN Red

List of Threatened Species, other national and international lists of threatened animals (e.g., Zoo Taxon lists and lists from societies specializing in particular taxa), and group member's expertise and specialist knowledge will all be used to produce a final order of priorities for sample collection. Groups will assess the time scales likely to be involved, and how best to gather, transport and store the samples. The level at which these groups operate, and their affiliations with other established national and international institutions around the world, such as the Taxon Advisory Groups, IUCN, the International Species Information Service (ISIS), the Conservation Breeding Specialist Group (CBSG) and the Amphibian Ark, will be determined by circumstance and opportunity.

In the United Kingdom, the first Taxon Expert Group (for land molluscs) has been set up with curators at the NHM and biologists at Nottingham. The Wildlife Heritage Trust of Sri Lanka, supported by the Darwin Initiative, is also involved. This Mollusc Expert Group is serving as something of a test bed for the development of others. At the LIRANS Institute of Applied Naturals Sciences at the University of Bedfordshire, a group is being developed for marine fish. ZSL, in collaboration with San Diego Zoo and the Amphibian Ark (McGregor Reid & Zippel, 2008), is developing one for the amphibians. A group for the corals is in the planning stage.

The Database

Essential for all aspects of the Frozen Ark is the construction of a database of a sort described by Hanner & Gregory (2007), which is needed for all biodiversity repositories. It will hold information about material stored by consortium members and others around the world that hold samples of threatened species for the collection that have been stored in appropriate ways. The information will enable a global list of the animals currently most in need of sampling to be produced. The database, which will be made available to all consortium members through password access, will have appropriately built-in safeguards to protect intellectual property rights, to provide secure information exchange and to allow provision for those wishing to contribute numerical data only. Additional arrangements for confidentiality can be drafted into individual memoranda where required.

The information collected about samples includes the taxonomic data, numbers of accessions, places of collection, pedigree data (from zoo studbooks), those responsible for the collection, numbers of samples, details of preservation and storage, and the presence or absence of voucher specimens and bar codes. Summary lists will be open to all interested parties outside the consortium who supply lists of their own collections. These arrangements will determine what has already been preserved and enable an assessment of the magnitude of the task ahead.

The data will be converted into a common format compatible with other relevant databases, such as those used by museums, the DNA genome programmes and the proposed new Zoological Information Management System (ISIS/ZIMS) for animals maintained by the world's zoos. Meanwhile, we are compiling the database using an Excel system based on sample information sent to us in many different forms. We plan that eventually each organization with Frozen Ark samples will create, maintain and update details of their own collections directly onto the database using remote input via the Internet.

THE ROLE OF ZOOS AND AQUARIUMS

The creation of *The World Zoo and Aquarium Conservation Strategy* document has given zoos and aquariums around the world a mandate that puts conservation projects, both within zoos and in the wild, firmly on the agenda (WAZA, 2005). This blueprint for the long-term conservation role of zoos is to be followed by directed policies and manuals to help in achieving its aims. We hope that after a suitable development phase, an additional item of policy will be added: a request for members of WAZA's zoos and aquariums to collect samples from their resident threatened animals for the Frozen Ark collections. This could perhaps be suitable for inclusion under the banner of the activity of 'integrated conservation'.

The developing association between the Frozen Ark and zoos and aquariums could be a major force in the successful collection, distribution and use of genetic material for conservation-breeding programmes. We hope it will open up the opportunity for institutions to access gametes and tissues preserved around the world. It will facilitate contacts with museum taxonomists (to identify animals) and research scientists (for advice on setting up facilities and research programmes). Funding from international sources for all parties is likely to be benefited. Members of the veterinary committee of WAZA are involved in taking this developing association forward.

In zoos and aquariums, samples can be taken *postmortem* as well as from living animals, and from a variety of sources including ♂ and ♀ gametes, testes, ovaries, embryos, surplus animals (e.g., tadpoles), tissues, feathers, hairs, body fluids and buccal smears. From the mammals, umbilical cord and placental tissue samples can be acquired (if problems such as disturbing mother-infant bonding can be overcome) with no invasion of the animal. Noninvasive sampling minimizes requirements for special licences, although local legal requirements will have to be followed in each country.

Noninvasive sampling minimizes requirements for special licenses.

In the United Kingdom, Defra (Department for Environment, Food and Rural Affairs) has stated in its framework for the *Secretary of State's Standards of Modern Zoo Practice*

(Appendix 5 Veterinary Facilities) that zoo veterinarians should have, wherever possible, a 'duty of care' to collect samples from animals *postmortem* for institutions that request them (Defra, 2000).

Veterinarians and other staff at Twycross Zoo are currently engaged in carrying out a trial to test out our procedures and protocols for sampling from live and *postmortem* zoo animals, temporary storage of samples, their transport to a long-term repository and the collection of necessary data. When completed, these will be circulated initially to zoos in the United Kingdom, then to Europe and those in the wider world who are prepared to collect samples for the Frozen Ark Project.

An important aim of the programme over the next 3 years will be to sample as many of the 500 or so IUCN-listed threatened species currently held by British zoos and aquariums.

The success of the Frozen Ark Project will depend on the help of zoos and aquariums worldwide.

SAMPLES STORED

To date, members of the Frozen Ark Consortium have stored material from more than 200 threatened species. They include over 30 that are extinct in the wild. In the United Kingdom, material for the DNA collection is being held in −80 °C freezers (soon to be in liquid nitrogen) in Nottingham and the NHM. Mammalian cells for tissue culture are being collected, prepared and stored in liquid nitrogen at the IoZ. Fish tissues and cell cultures are being prepared and stored in liquid nitrogen at the University of Bedfordshire. Outside the United Kingdom, samples are held by consortium members at San Diego Zoo and the American Museum of Natural History (United States), at Monash University and Perth Zoo (Australia), at the National Zoo in Pretoria (South Africa), at Auckland Zoo (New Zealand) and at the Centre for Cellular and Molecular Biology in Hyderabad (India).

For institutions wanting to set up their own collection of DNA, tissues or cells, an excellent model for a dedicated facility can be found at the Ambrose Monell Cryobank web site (http://www.research.amnh.org). It is a useful introduction to the subject, provides protocols on sample collection, advises how to set up a frozen facility, to care for the collection, to manage data records and to maintain the storage of samples (Corthals & DeSalle, 2005).

The preservation of genetic resources within bio-banks provides a secure *ex situ* method for keeping the genomes and viable cells of threatened species. The success of the Frozen Ark Project will depend on the help of zoos and aquariums worldwide. They are essential because of their ability to collect tissues and cell samples from animals in their care. As the number of threatened species grows exponentially, zoos and aquariums are increasingly in the unique position of being the major organizations that will have access to this material.

Acknowledgements

I am grateful to Professor Bryan Clarke for much discussion and for his useful suggestions on the manuscript, and to Ms Jude Smith for her excellent administrative assistance.

REFERENCES

Andrabi, S. M. H. & Maxwell, W. M. C. (2007): A review on reproductive biotechnologies for conservation of endangered mammal species. *Animal Reproductive Science* 99: 223–243.

Benford, G. (1992): Saving the library of life. *Proceedings of the National Academy of Sciences of the United States of America* 89: 11098–11101.

Benirschke, K. (1984): The frozen zoo concept. *Zoo Biology* 3: 325–328.

Chao, H., Davies, P. L. & Carpenter, J. F. (1996): Effects of antifreeze proteins on red blood cell survival during cryo-preservation. *The Journal of Experimental Biology* 199: 2071–2076.

Clarke, A. G. (2006): The Frozen Ark Project. In *ARAZPA Annual Conference 2006. Integration: the challenge for conservation.* Perth, Australia: ARAZPA. http://www.arazpa.org.au/2006-ARAZPA-Conference-Proceedings/default.aspx

Clarke, A. G. (2007): The Frozen Ark Project. In *WAZA Conferences: Proceedings of the 62nd Annual Meeting, hosted by Budapest Zoo, 26–30 August 2007: links between ex situ and in situ conservation of native species*: 186–187. Bern: WAZA.

Clarke, A. G. & Rawson, D. (2007): Workshop on the Frozen Ark Project. In *WAZA Conferences: Proceedings of the 62nd Annual Meeting, hosted by Budapest Zoo, 26–30 August 2007: links between ex situ and in situ conservation of native species*: 225–227. Bern: WAZA.

Corthals, A. & DeSalle, R. (2005): An application of tissue and DNA banking for genomics and conservation: the Ambrose Monell Cryo-Collection (AMCC). *Systematic Biology* 54: 819–823.

Crowe, J. H. & Crowe, L. M. (2000): Preservation of mammalian cells: learning nature's tricks. *Nature Biotechnology* 18: 145–146.

Defra (2000): *Secretary of State's standards of modern zoo practice.* London: Defra. http://www.defra.gov.uk/ wildlife-countryside/gwd/zooprac/pdf/zooprac.pdf

Dessauer, H. C., COLE, C. J. & HAFNER, M. S. (1996): Collection and storage of tissues. In *Molecular systematics* (2nd edn). 29–47. Hillis, D. M., Moritz, C. M. & Mable, B. K. (Eds). Sunderland, MA: Sinauer Associates.

Dobrinski, I. & Travis, A. J. (2007): Germ cell transplantation for the propagation of companion animals, nondomestic & endangered species. *Reproduction, Fertility and Development* 19: 732–739.

Dresser, B. L., Gelwicks, E. J., Wachs, K. B. & Keller, G. L. (1988): First successful transfer of cryopreserved feline (*Felis catus*) embryos resulting in live offspring. *Journal of Experimental Zoology* 246: 180–186.

Fogarty, N. M., Maxwell, W. M. C., Eppleston, J. & Evans, G. (2000): The viability of transferred sheep embryos after long term cryopreservation. *Reproduction, Fertility and Development* 12: 31–37.

Gomez, M. C., Pope, C. E. & Dresser, B. L. (2007): Nuclear transfer in cats and its application. *Theriogenology* 66: 72–81.

Guan, M., Rawson, D. M. & Zhang, T. (2008): Cryopreservation of zebrafish (Danio rerio) oocytes using improved controlled slow cooling protocols. *Cryobiology* 56: 204–208.

Hanner, R. H. & Gregory, T. R. (2007): Genomic diversity research and the role of biorepositories. *Cell Preservation Technology* 5: 93–103.

Holt, W. V. (2008): Cryobiology. Wildlife conservation and reality. *Cryobiology* 29: 3–52.

Holt, W. V., Bennett, P. M., Volobouev, V. & Watson, P. F. (1996): Genetic resource banks in wildlife conservation. *Journal of Zoology*, London 238: 531–544.

Hoss, M., Jaruga, P., Zastawny, T. H., Dizdaroglu, M. & Paabo, S. (1996): DNA damage and DNA sequence retrieval from ancient tissues. *Nucleic Acids Research* 24: 1304–1307.

IUCN (2007): *2007 IUCN red list of threatened species.* Gland, Switzerland, and Cambridge, UK: IUCN. http:// www.iucnredlist.org/ (downloaded 4 May 2008).

Kammenga, J. E., Herman, M. A., Ouborg, N. J. O., Johnson, L. & Breitling, R. (2007): Microarray challenges in ecology. *Trends in Ecology and Evolution* 22: 273–279.

Lee, K. (2001): Can cloning save endangered species? *Current Biology* 11: 245–246.

Lindahl, T. (1993): Instability and decay of the primary structure of DNA. *Nature* 362: 709–715.

Linington, S. H. (2000): The Millennium Seed Bank Project. In *Biological collections and biodiversity.* Linnean Society occasional papers 3: 358–373. Rushton, B. S., Hackney, P. & Tyne, C. R. (Eds). Otley: Westbury Publishing and London: Linnean Society.

Loi, P., Ptak, G., Barboni, B., Fulka JR, J., Cappai, P. & Clinton, M. (2001): Genetic rescue of an endangered mammal by cross-species nuclear transfer using postmortem somatic cells. *Nature Biotechnology* 19: 962–964.

Mastromonaco, G. F. & Allan King, W. (2007): Cloning in companion animals, non-domestic and endangered species: can the technology become a practical reality? *Reproduction, Fertility and Development* 19: 745–761.

May, R. M. (1988): How many species are here on earth? *Science* 241: 1441–1449.

Mazur, P., Cole, K.W., Hall, J.W., Schreuders, P.D. & Mahowald, A. P. (1992): Cryobiological preservation of Drosophila embryos. *Science* 258: 1932–1935.

McGregor Reid, G. & Zippel, K. C. (2008): Can zoos and aquariums ensure the survival of amphibians in the 21st century? *International Zoo Yearbook* 42: 1–6.

Millennium Ecosystem Assessment (2005): *Ecosystems and human well-being: biodiversity synthesis*. Washington, DC: World Resources Institute.

Poinar, H. N., Schwarz, C., QI, J., Shapiro, B., MacPhee, R. D. E., Buigues, B., Tikhonov, A., Huson, D. H., Tomsho, L. P., Auch, A., Rampp, M., Miller, W. & Schuster, S. C. (2006): Metagenomics to paleogenomics: large-scale sequencing of mammoth DNA. *Science* 311: 392–394

Pukazhenthi, B., Comizzoli, P., Travis, A. J. & Wildt, D. E. (2006): Applications in emerging technologies to the study and conservation of threatened and endangered species. *Reproduction, Fertility and Development* 18: 77–90.

Ryder, O. A. & Benirschke, K. (1997): The potential of "cloning" in the conservation effort. *Zoo Biology* 16: 295–300.

Ryder, O. A., McLaren, A., Brenner, S., Zhang, Y.-P. & Benirschke, K. (2000): DNA banks for endangered animal species. *Science* 288: 275–277.

Service, R. E. (2006): The race for the $1000 genome. *Science* 311: 1544–1546.

Smith, L.M. & Burgoyne, L. A. (2001): Species identity: conserved inverted LINE repeat clusters (ILRC) in the vertebrate genome as indicators of population boundaries. *Gene* 271: 273–283.

Stoughton, R. B. (2005): Applications of DNA microarrays in biology. *Annual Review of Biochemistry* 74: 53–82.

Thomas, C. D., Cameron, A., Green, R. E., Bakkenes, M., Beaumont, L. J., Collingham, Y. C., Erasmus, B., Ferreira de Siqueira, M., Grainger, A., Hannah, L., Hughes, L., Huntly, B., van Jaarsveld, A. S., Midgley, G. F., Miles, L., Ortega-Huerta, M. A., Peterson, A. T., Phillips, O. L. & Williams, S. E. (2004): Extinction rates from climate change. *Nature* 427: 145–148.

UNEP (2008): Biodiversity. In GEO-4 – *global environment outlook: environment for development*: 157–192. Nairobi, Kenya: United Nations Environment Programme. http://www.unep.org/geo/geo4/report/GEO-4_ Report_Full_en.pdf

Vink, C. J., Thomas, S. M., Paquin, P., Hayashi, C. Y. & Hedin, M. (2005): The effects of preservatives and temperatures on arachnid DNA. *Invertebrate Systematics* 19: 99–104.

WAZA (2005): *Building a future for wildlife. The world zoo and aquarium conservation strategy*. Bern: WAZA. http://www.waza.org/conservation/wzacs.php

Wells, D. N., Pavla, P. M., Tervit, H. R. & Vivanco, W. H. (1998): Adult somatic cell nuclear transfer is used to preserve the last surviving cow of the Enderby Island cattle breed. *Reproduction, Fertility and Development* 10: 369–378.

Wilmut, I., Schnieke, A. E., McWhir, J., Kind, A. J. & Campbell, K H. S. (1997): Viable offspring derived from fetal and adult mammalian cells. *Nature* 385: 810–813.

Zhang, T. & Rawson, D. M. (2002): Studies on cryopreservation of LUC gene transfected bluegill sunfish fibroblast cell line. *Cryoletters* 23: 191–196.

Bolivian Circus Animals Are in Limbo After a Ban on Keeping Wild Animals

Carlos Valdez

In the following viewpoint, Associated Press writer Carlos Valdez reports on the status of Bolivian circus animals following a ban on wild animals performing in such events. The Bolivian government abolished the exhibition of circus animals, which has led to a crisis for animal rights activists. These animals are expensive to feed and house, and they require special trainers to care for them. Nonetheless, Valdez writes, the effort is worth the cost for most advocates because the circus conditions were deplorable.

As you read, consider the following questions:

1. What does Valdez estimate as a lion's life span in the wild?

2. According to Susana Carpio, why was the law banning the exhibition of wild animals in Bolivia passed?

3. How many pounds of red meat do the rescued lions eat per week?

She could have lived till 40 in the wild, where the average life span of a lion is double that in captivity. But Maiza is

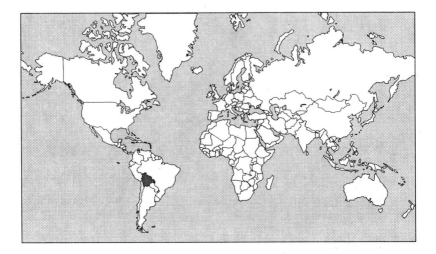

frail and nearly blind after 18 years in the circus, jumping through flaming hoops and performing at the point of trainer's whip.

Two of her cubs had their fangs cut for trainers who wow crowds by sticking their heads inside lions' mouths. Another, not Maiza's, had her claws ripped out at birth—without anesthetic.

Such stories of abuse, along with clandestine circus videos made by animal rights activists, prompted Bolivia to enact the world's most comprehensive circus-animal ban.

While some European countries already prohibit the exhibition of wild animals in circuses, the Bolivian ban covers domestic animals and pets as well.

Absorbing Care Costs

Maiza, four cubs and a baboon, Tillin, will be early beneficiaries of the law that takes effect in July [2010]. The five cats are headed next month [May 2010] to a California refuge for former animal performers, while the baboon is expected to be housed in a special sanctuary in Britain.

The fate remains uncertain, however, for dozens of other animals in small circuses roaming the country. Neither authorities nor advocacy groups know what they will do with creatures that—like Maiza—are given up or seized. Zoos already are too crowded and, apart from [the capital city] La Paz's, substandard.

The cost of caring for the five lions and baboon so far is double the estimated budget.

"I don't dare give an amount," said Enrique Mendizabal of Animal Defenders International, or ADI, a Britain-based group that fought for the ban and has committed to support Maiza and the others.

The cost of caring for the five lions and baboon so far is double the estimated budget.

Though circus operators were given a year to comply, owner Salvador Abuhadba gave up the cats and baboon last August, saying he didn't want trouble from the new law.

"They were part of my family . . . they deserve a dignified retirement," said Abuhadba, who denies they were abused and has renamed his animal-free operation Abuhadba's Ecological Circus.

"I don't make the money I used to. People are fascinated with circus animals. But I think I did the right thing."

Deplorable Conditions

The animals' new caretakers say they were fed Coca-Cola, chicken scraps and leftovers. They suspect the baboon has diabetes and are working with a primate expert in Britain to try to find out.

Behind the fantasy, illusion and entertainment, the circus hides a life of animal cruelty, said Susana Carpio of Bolivian-based Animales S.O.S.

A hippopotamus died in his sleep when his circus pool froze over in the Andean city of Potosi, 13,123 feet above sea level. A dwarf elephant was killed by La Paz's harsh climate in 2007.

Circuses That Travel Compromise Animal Welfare

The travelling circus is not a suitable environment for an animal, because restrictions of space, time, mobility of equipment and facilities mean that no animal will be able to behave as it would in its natural environment. Many of the species commonly kept in circuses have highly specialised behaviour, making it impossible to cater for them in the circus.

We acknowledge that suffering in both humans and animals is difficult to prove. However if animals are behaving in a way that would give rise to concern were they any other species, then we should assume that such concern is justified until proven otherwise; it should be a reflection of a humane society to allow the potential victims the benefit of the doubt.

Animal Defenders International,
"Animals in Travelling Circuses:
The Science on Suffering," 2006.

"The death of the elephant Rossi moved us to press for the law," Carpio said.

That same year, ADI infiltrated circus workers in Bolivia, Peru, Ecuador and Colombia and filmed videos of the animals chained and crowded in cages barely bigger than they were, living in their own feces, Mendizabal said.

If they resisted their trainers, they would be beaten. Elephants were made to do their tricks with hooks stuck in their skin, according to ADI video viewed by the Associated Press.

The same images were given to Bolivian legislators.

"It took two years to pass the law. Some senators feared the next step would be to ban bullfighting that's very popular in the eastern villages," said former legislator Ximena Flores, who sponsored the bill.

Carpio said it was possible to pass the law because Bolivia has no strong circus lobby, only medium- and small-tent operations that keep their animals in poor conditions. ADI is pushing similar initiatives in other countries and says it has made the most headway so far in Peru.

The animals' new caretakers say they were fed Coca-Cola, chicken scraps and leftovers.

Shortly after the Bolivia law passed last July, Abuhadba called Animales S.O.S. to come pick up his brood.

"They opened the cage and gave them to me," Carpio said. "I didn't know what to do with them. I didn't have a leash to take them as if they were pets."

The animals were confined to their circus cages until ADI constructed a secure refuge for them in a Cochabamba park, where neighbors at first complained about the roaring and feared the lions could escape.

There are no wild-animal experts in Bolivia. ADI had to import a specialist in large felines to evaluate and monitor the health of the rescued animals.

Subjugated their whole lives, the lions don't have the grandeur or courage of their counterparts that dominate the African savanna. But a good diet, nutritional supplements and painstaking care have allowed them to recover some weight and animal instincts.

They each devour a total of 80–100 pounds of red meat during three feedings a week.

But circuses from surrounding countries no longer travel to Bolivia for fear their animals will be seized.

Canadian and American Puppy Mills Must Be Shut Down

Mary-Jo Dionne

In the following viewpoint Mary-Jo Dionne, a writer based in Vancouver, Canada, argues that the conditions of Canadian and American puppy mills are appalling. Dogs are kept in small cages with little food and water, she asserts. Furthermore, the canines are often dirty and neglected. Unlike reputable breeders who specialize in the welfare of select breeds, mills specialize in producing as many puppies as possible, as cheaply as possible, the author argues. Dionne encourages people interested in adopting dogs to turn not to puppy mills but to private breeders and animal shelters.

As you read, consider the following questions:

1. About how many puppies does Dionne assert can be sold on a weekly basis by some puppy mills?
2. Puppy mill operators might work with how many breeds of dogs, according to the viewpoint?
3. How many puppies do American pet stores sell annually, in PIJAC's estimate?

Mary-Jo Dionne, "Puppy Hell: The Horrors of Puppy Mills," *Modern Dog Magazine*, Winter 2005–2006. Copyright © 2005–2006 by *Modern Dog Inc.* Reproduced by permission.

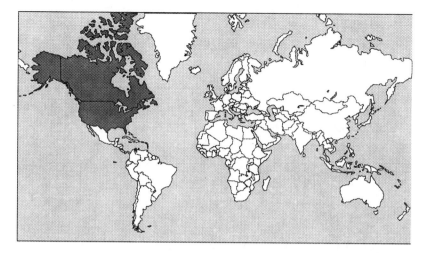

The term "puppy love" conjures images of teen couples passing notes in the school hallway. All is warm and fuzzy. The term "puppy dog eyes" brings to mind big, droopy, please-love-me peepers reflecting innocence and loyalty. Both of these colloquialisms are made all the more appealing by virtue of one simple word: "puppy." Not only have we come to love the sweet little creatures themselves, but—let's face it—we love the word. Puppy.

Perhaps it is this image of gentleness coupled with the jovial cadence of a word we love that has served to mask one of society's most disgusting realities. For those not in the know, the phrase "puppy mill" might conjure nothing more than an animated, cartoonesque conveyor belt, spewing out tail-wagging baby dogs. From an *I Love Lucy* [a TV show from the 1950s] bon-bon factory environment right into the arms of loving families. For many, little more thought is given to the idea of "puppy mill" as a place of dog origin than is given to the idea of "stork" as baby origin. Perhaps if we replaced "puppy mill" with a more apt phrase—"torture chamber"—we'd finally be able to stand up and say: "Okay, now I get it." Maybe then our cocktail-party chatter would be less about the dog-du-jour [dog of the day] and more about the responsible adoption of, and lifetime commitment to, the dog-de-la-vie [dog for life].

Puppy mills create living conditions for their dogs that are deplorable at best.

What Is a Puppy Mill?

Let's start by getting that quaint old tune out of our heads and stop asking, "How much is that doggie in the window?" Instead, we should be asking, "Where did that doggie in the window come from?" And more specifically, "If I purchase that doggie in the window, what is my money supporting?" Because, quite simply, if the window in which that doggie sits is one belonging to a pet store, more than likely, that doggie came from a puppy mill. In a 2004 article in the *Province*, BC SPCA [British Columbia Society for the Prevention of Cruelty to Animals] senior animal-protection officer Eileen Drever explained: "It's a fact that reputable breeders will not allow their puppies to be sold through pet stores."

As defined by Canada's National Companion Animal Coalition, a "puppy mill" is a high-volume, substandard dog breeding operation which sells purebred or mixed-breed dogs. Facilities that mass-produce puppies and put profit above welfare, puppy mills create living conditions for their dogs that are deplorable at best.

Picture, if you will, a warehouse. Imagine, within this warehouse, row after row and shelf after shelf of inventory stuffed into cramped, makeshift cages. The "inventory" in each box is half a dozen or more puppies, frequently hungry, sickly, and covered in the feces of the "inventory" shelved above them. And above them.

But wait. Those conditions are the Club Med of the mill. However neglected these puppies are, their stay will likely be short, given that some mills sell up to 150 puppies a week. The suffering is not so temporary for the lifers. The "breeding stock" animals are imprisoned in overcrowded, filthy cages and repetitively bred—even inbred—until they simply no longer can, often without ever experiencing the luxury of leaving their cages. Minimal vet care, poor-quality food, and small living quarters make up the sub-substandard conditions in which countless mothers give birth to hundreds of thousands of puppies yearly.

A puppy mill is the rude, ugly, hateful cousin of the companion-pet world.

While a reputable breeder will work with one or two breeds in order to fully understand and care for her puppies, a puppy mill operator may crank out up to seventy different breeds. When the mandate is to produce as many puppies as you can, as fast as you can, and as cheaply as you can, puppy mill dogs are reduced to the status of widgets. According to Stephanie Shain, director of the Stop Puppy Mills Campaign for the Humane Society of the United States (HSUS): "Legally, if individuals treated their pets the way dogs in puppy mills are treated, they could be charged with cruelty or neglect. But these mills are viewed as 'agriculture' and too often, the agencies responsible for overseeing them treat them like they are raising corn, not pets."

In 2000, a particularly horrendous case uncovered in Quebec [Canada] infuriated the nation. The mill was littered with piles of dead, partially eaten dogs, in corners, behind the barn, and even hanging from rafters. Starving adult dogs were found eating their newborn puppies.

So, what is a puppy mill? A puppy mill is the rude, ugly, hateful cousin of the companion-pet world. The cousin who runs the risk of tarnishing the reputation of every member of the family, even the well-meaning ones. The cousin whose branch you wish you could chop from the family tree.

The Dogs in Our Own Backyards

Perhaps the biggest barrier that stands between North Americans and puppy mill reality is our distorted perception of self. The Canadian and American public blithely believes that puppy mills couldn't possibly be as bad as "they" say. Because, we're civilized, right?

As civilized as the man who stuffed five young Rottweiler puppies into a birdcage and left them there. Naturally, but tragically, these puppies continued to grow and, eventually, too large to be extracted from the cage, had to be euthanized through its bars. This didn't happen in some far-off Third World country but in our own, tidy North American backyard.

What can be done to punish millers like this one? The first stumbling block in bringing operators to justice is that they actually have to be found, and this is not an industry that works in plain view. In Canada, animal welfare laws differ from province to province. While the law allows for penalties as severe as a $60,000 fine and two years in prison, such sentences are rarely handed down. As Pierre Barnoti, executive director of the SPCA in Quebec explains, in his twelve years with the organization, he has never seen a puppy mill operator serve so much as one day of time.

Barnoti has become an oft-heard and respected voice in the fight for the eradication of puppy mills. He is quick to point out the irony that, at 136 years old, Quebec's SPCA is the oldest in Canada, yet, up until only months ago, it was the only province with no animal welfare act in place. A mere nine animal welfare inspectors struggle to oversee a geographic area approximately six times the size of France. As such, it is a haven for puppy millers, supplying more dogs to North American pet stores than any other province or state.

South of the border, Shain estimates that there are easily over 5,000 mills in operation. While some local shelters and governmental agencies do investigate puppy mill conditions and intervene to rescue the animals, in many cases, it's unclear whether the shelter has the legal authority to step in. Even when they can take action, the magnitude of the situation is often so overwhelming that solving it becomes a monumental task. When a shelter intervenes, they suddenly find themselves with dozens of animals in need of care, housing, and food. A rescue of as few as fifty dogs can cost tens of thousands of dollars.

Unfortunately, puppy mills are more than slipping through cracks. They are plummeting through craters.

A rescue of as few as fifty dogs can cost tens of thousands of dollars.

The Burden Is Ours

How could something like this not only continue but thrive as a profitable industry?

The answer is simple: Because of us—consumers who walk into pet stores empty-handed, and walk out with a new designer dog. Or who see an ad in the paper and hours later pick up a puppy. Who surf the net [Internet] and—wowed by irresistible photos—order up a dog as if it were a book or bouquet of flowers. In our obsession with having a "purebred" and having it quickly, we feed the industry. Pet stores cater to impulsive buyers seeking convenient transactions.

On the other hand, reputable breeders and shelters care where their puppies go. Alison Brownlie recently became the mom of Taz, a Border Collie-cross rescued from the Vancouver-based That'll Do Border Collie Rescue. Describing the screening she underwent before adopting Taz, she says: "The application process was incredibly thorough. Once my application was approved, a volunteer came to do a home check. Only after these two filters did I even get to meet him! Then, I had to wait another 24 hours before the adoption would be confirmed. The objective of the shelter is: No snap decisions! This isn't about a new stuffed toy, this is about a possible 15-year friendship."

"There is one really easy way to stop puppy mills. And that is not to buy the puppies."

Breed-specific rescue groups like the one that sheltered Taz exist continent-wide to help match up potential owners with dogs that need homes. In addition, it is a little-known fact that a quarter of all the dogs in shelters are purebreds, so even if you want a purebred, there is no need to buy the dog of your dreams from a pet store when countless are sitting un-loved in shelters.

The Pet Industry Joint Advisory Council (PIJAC) estimates that American pet stores alone sell between 300,000 and 400,000 puppies a year. If you estimate something in the range of $500 paid per pet store puppy, that's an astounding amount of money directly supporting the puppy mill system. No won-der puppy mill operators look at dogs not as "man's best friend" but as "man's best cash cow." And the cash is ours. As Shain says: "Puppy mill operators count on people to be so overwhelmed by the cuteness that they just can't leave the little bundle behind. But people must understand when they take the puppy home, they've opened up a space for the next one to fill." Put bluntly: "There is one really easy way to stop puppy mills. And that is not to buy the puppies."

Ignorance is not bliss. We can [no] longer wince at cock-tail parties: "Oh no, I can't hear about it." We must hear about it. We must turn our backs on anyone who cannot tell us where that doggie in the window came from. We must be able to say: "Okay, now I get it."

When it comes to putting the innocence back in the word "puppy," the burden is entirely ours.

Ireland Must Develop a System for Tracking Horse Ownership and Well-Being

Joe Collins, et al.

Joe Collins is a member and the outgoing president of Veterinary Ireland, as well as a veterinary practioner in Ireland. In the following viewpoint, he and his colleagues argue that more considerations need to be made for the welfare of horses in Ireland. As the sports and leisure equine industry grows, it becomes even more important for horses to be properly tracked and maintained. Not only does Ireland risk economic losses, but lack of attention to horses used in this industry can also lead to mistreatment and death.

As you read, consider the following questions:

1. About how many sports and leisure horses does the viewpoint estimate there are per thousand people in Ireland?

2. What policy sets the legislative standard for animal welfare in Ireland?

3. During what year did Ireland experience an outbreak of equine infectious anemia in the horse population?

Joe Collins, et al., "The Structure and Regulation of the Irish Equine Industries: Links to Considerations of Equine Welfare," *Irish Veterinary Journal*, vol. 61, no. 11, November 2008, pp. 746, 752–755. Copyright © 2008 by IFP Media. Reproduced by permission.

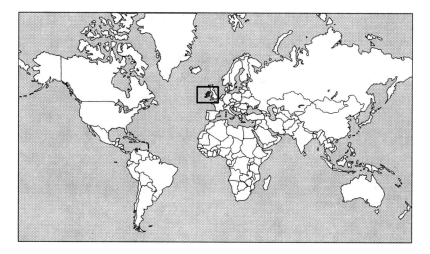

The equine industries in Ireland have been vibrant and growing. Total thoroughbred (TB) horse sales at public auction in Ireland grew in value by 31.5% in one year alone from €145,626 [euros] in 2005 to€&191,463 in 2006. The numbers of TB foals registered and horses returned in training has grown by 17.5% (from 10,214 to 12,004) and 22% (from 9,080 to 11,109), respectively, over the five years to 2006. In contrast, in 2007 as compared to 2006, although there has been a further 9.7% increase in the numbers of horses returned in training (from 11,109 to 12,188), there has been a 7% decrease (from a record €189.4 million in 2006) in the value of bloodstock sales at public auction. This latter figure is a sensitive indicator of current confidence in the market for young horses, and thus future trends for older animals. There are an estimated 27.5 sports/leisure horses per thousand people (the most horse-dense population in Europe), highlighting the importance of equestrianism in Ireland.

The role of animal welfare within the equine industries has gained increasing prominence internationally. Animal use is generally accepted by society, provided that the benefits associated with this use do not outweigh harm to the animals. When we use animals, we take on a moral obligation towards those animals. This duty of care is informed by legislative provisions, codes of practice and guidelines aimed at safeguarding the health and welfare of animals. . . .

There are two broad sectors within the Irish equine industry. The majority of TB horses in Ireland are bred for racing—non-TB horses cannot be so used—and a discrete structure can be identified for the TB racing sector. Sports horses are defined as those of all breeds and types used for recreational and competitive purposes other than racing. . . .

The role of animal welfare within the equine industries has gained increasing prominence internationally.

Equine Welfare

People can enhance or diminish the standard of welfare for horses with which they interact. . . . The value placed by a person on a horse's welfare will depend on the type and intensity of the human-horse relationship, and how the personal costs of ownership are balanced against the perceived benefits. The human perception of animal welfare is undoubtedly affected by what the animal is used for and thus, the more valued the animal is, the more likely that the human influence will tend to improve the welfare standard. Where animals are valued primarily in an economic context there can be an inherent conflict between animal welfare (as perceived by humans) and livestock productivity (as pursued by increasingly 'intensive' methods of production). Another method of grading an animal's value to us is to place it on a socio-zoologic scale, where 'good' animals rank highly as pets or companions; those with some extrinsic value to us occupy middle ranking as tools; and pests, vermin and others considered to represent a nuisance or threat are assigned the lowest status. . . .

Animal welfare science is a poorly funded research discipline in Ireland. This is especially the case with equine welfare, reflected by the small number of peer-reviewed publications. In spite of the limited framework supporting horse welfare in Ireland, the horse industries understand that they have a general responsibility to ensure the health and welfare of horses they use. It is also vital to the organising bodies that the general public [is] convinced that the training, competition and management practices used are not in any way abusive. In a report commissioned by the Irish Horse Board, these authors identified areas in which standards may be compromised and listed recommendations for the safeguarding of equine welfare. Horse Sport Ireland has appointed a training and education manager who will have responsibility for coordinating this approach to improving welfare standards. Comprehensive animal welfare guidelines for horses, donkeys and ponies in Ireland have been developed by an advisory council to the Minister for Agriculture, Fisheries and Food. Currently, the legislative standard for animal welfare in the ROI [Republic of Ireland] is that as set down in the UK [United Kingdom] Protection of Animals Act of 1911, although in more recent years, regulations have emanated from the EU [European Union] establishing a framework of legal provisions concerning food-producing species and animals used in research. In 2008, equines (except while being used in competitions, shows, cultural and sporting events) were brought within the scope of EU legislation designed to protect the welfare of farmed animals obliging a person to ensure that an animal under [his] care is not caused unnecessary pain, suffering or injury. . . .

The human perception of animal welfare is undoubtedly affected by what the animal is used for.

Evidence-Based Research Is Needed

There are a number of fundamental issues that adversely compromise the health and welfare status of horses in Ireland.

Each is underpinned by concerns relating to equine identification and the registration of ownership. It is not currently possible to track horses from birth to death, except those whose owners/keepers voluntarily register their origin, change of ownership, movement and ultimate demise. There is no legally enforced system of mandatory registration of horses, their place of keeping or their ownership. The export and import of horses are not effectively monitored. With at least 8% of members of a large sports horse breeders' cooperative admitting keeping unregistered mares, it is highly likely that others, who are not members of any equestrian organisation or registered with the CSO [Central Statistics Office] as farm owners, will possess unregistered horses in even greater percentages. Issues that depend on a coherent and comprehensive system cannot be legally enforced. There has been little formal study or discussion of these further issues to date. The chief executive of Horse Racing Ireland has warned that "horses were currently being produced for which there would be no races." There must be evidence-based research to provide objective data on the numbers, types, suitability, uses and endpoints of horses produced.

Disposal of Horses. The number of horses being processed for the human food chain, taken in combination with the number being disposed of legally via the registered knackery system and veterinary laboratories, is at variance with the numbers of horses being produced. Excepting those horses processed by the sole licensed horse slaughter facility, there is no system of recording when horses leave the population by death or transport abroad. Many are falling through the gaps in the industry structures, and being unaccounted for, which represents a real or potential threat to equine welfare. For example, it is commonly held that licenses are not sought for the disposal of horses by burial in remote areas.

Disease Surveillance. An outbreak of equine infectious anaemia [anemia] in the horse population in Ireland in 2006 has served as a wake-up call to the government and the equine industries about how ill prepared we might be if a more contagious disease entered our immunologically naïve population of horses. AHS [African horse sickness] and WNV [West Nile virus] may represent such threats to our equine population and to our equine industries.

Currently, the registered owner of an animal is not necessarily the legal owner.

Both can cause high morbidity and mortality rates in susceptible populations, raising serious welfare concerns for our horse population, were we unable, due to lack of a rigorous identification and tracing system for horses, to contain an outbreak.

Registration and Identification

Medicine Use. Animal remedies regulations depend, for their implementation regarding horses, on a reliable system of identification of equidae. Horses are classified in EU legislation as a 'food-producing animal' unless otherwise specifically declared by the owner. The financial turnover of the veterinary medicines market is reported to be only 3–5% of the pharmaceutical market, with more than 50% of the market involving the agriculture sector and profit margins smaller than in the human sector. As the market in licensed veterinary medicinal products progressively contracts due to the cost of the licensing procedure (particularly a problem when studying medicines for equidae) and the relatively small available market, the importance of innovative, non-equine licensed veterinary and human remedies becomes ever greater for safeguarding equine welfare. These non-equine licensed medicines must be

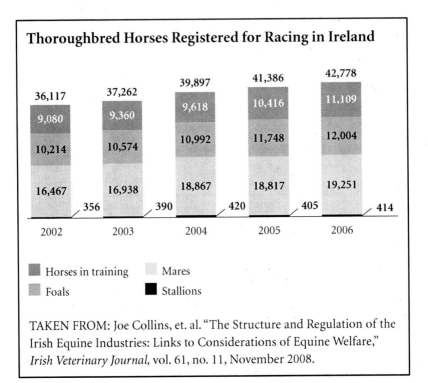

Thoroughbred Horses Registered for Racing in Ireland

	2002	2003	2004	2005	2006
Total	36,117	37,262	39,897	41,386	42,778
Horses in training	9,080	9,360	9,618	10,416	11,109
Mares	10,214	10,574	10,992	11,748	12,004
Foals	16,467	16,938	18,867	18,817	19,251
Stallions	356	390	420	405	414

Legend: Horses in training · Mares · Foals · Stallions

TAKEN FROM: Joe Collins, et. al. "The Structure and Regulation of the Irish Equine Industries: Links to Considerations of Equine Welfare," *Irish Veterinary Journal*, vol. 61, no. 11, November 2008.

used under the cascade system for nonfood-producing species with a requirement to permanently exclude the horse from the human food chain. This process relies on an ability to accurately identify the animal being treated, but encourages noncompliance with identification legislation due to the cost of disposal of nonfood designated horses.

Legal Responsibility for Owning and Keeping Horses. Currently the registered owner of an animal is not necessarily the legal owner, this has been based on owner self-certification at the time of registration. There is no legal responsibility to correctly register ownership or any subsequent change. An unknown number of horses remain unregistered. This presents serious legal difficulties when it becomes necessary to conduct a prosecution under animal welfare legislation. . . .

Transport. EU transport of animals regulations, as applied to equidae, which were implemented in 2007, were motivated by a desire to pressurise those engaged in the long-distance transport of horses for slaughter sufficiently so as to render this trade uneconomic. The work of groups such as Animals' Angels and the International League for the Protection of Horses (ILPH) in this regard continues. There is, however, increasing disquiet among the commercial horse transport sector that their ability to trade in non-slaughter horses has been unduly compromised. The increased requirements for driver training and certification, partitioning of horses, lodging of travel plans and satellite tracking of vehicles has undoubtedly introduced an additional layer of bureaucracy and cost. . . .

Ireland Must Commit to Equine Welfare

Horses are hugely valuable to Ireland on several levels—economic, social and individual. The success of industry sectors in positioning Ireland as a global force in the racing and sports horse business cannot be overestimated. Socially, culturally and traditionally horses have been interwoven with Irish society at a fundamental level. Similarly, the risks to Ireland's equine industries from a failure to appreciate the threats to equine health and welfare cannot be ignored. There are current and potential future problems with the horses themselves. The issue which underpins these threats is that of identification of horses, and the registration of horse ownership. The lack of a comprehensive integrated system of horse identification, and thus the other issues identified in this [viewpoint] which depend on it, fundamentally links current concerns for equine welfare. Research into these links is required, the findings should be disseminated appropriately so that those who are responsible for developing policy, those who manage the financial resources available to the equine industries, and those who are directly responsible for the horses themselves can be appropriately educated and the findings translated into actions that will nullify the threats and achieve real improvements in equine health and welfare.

The Australian Government Recommends That Primates Not Be Kept as Pets Outside Their Native Environments

National Consultative Committee on Animal Welfare (NCCAW)

National Consultative Committee on Animal Welfare (NCCAW) is a non-statutory body established in 1989 to advise on the effectiveness and appropriateness of national codes of practice, policies, guidelines, and legislation to safeguard and further the welfare of animals and protect the national interests. In the following viewpoint, the NCCAW states that primates should not be kept as pets because they have special needs and pose a danger to people and other animals. As a result, the NCCAW recommends that the practice of keeping primates as pets be phased out.

As you read, consider the following questions:

1. What needs of primates are unlikely to be met by their owners, according to the NCCAW?

2. What dangers do primates pose to other animals and to humans, according to the NCCAW?

National Consultative Committee on Animal Welfare (NCCAW), "Primates as Pets," National Guidelines for Animal Welfare, Australian Government, Department of Agriculture, Fisheries and Forestry. Copyright © Commonwealth of Australia 2011.

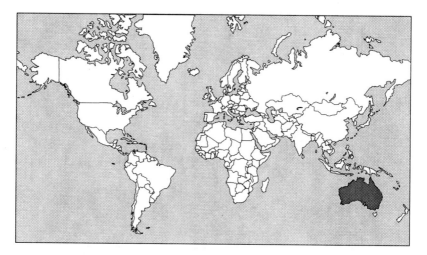

3. What conditions does the NCCAW impose on owners of primates, according to the viewpoint?

Primates such as monkey and chimpanzees are not suitable as pets because:

- their social needs, which include the company of other monkeys, cannot be met

- they need environmental enrichment and have strict requirements for housing, including security and access to the outdoors

---

[People keeping primates] should be able to demonstrate their knowledge of the species and its requirements, including diet, welfare, social and behavioural needs and so on.

- they can transfer serious diseases to humans

- the safety and welfare of other animals can be compromised if they escape, and

- they have complex dietary requirements that owners may not be aware of.

199

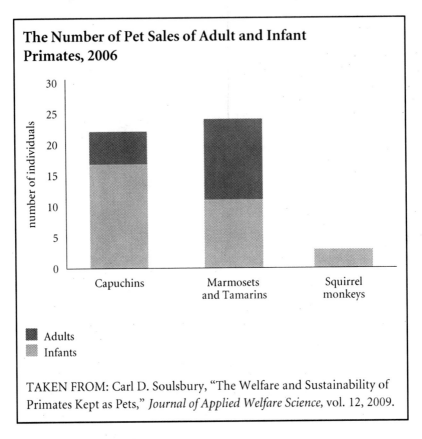

The Number of Pet Sales of Adult and Infant Primates, 2006

TAKEN FROM: Carl D. Soulsbury, "The Welfare and Sustainability of Primates Kept as Pets," *Journal of Applied Welfare Science,* vol. 12, 2009.

NCCAW's Position

People already keeping primates as pets should continue to do so, provided they meet strict standards for housing and welfare, and have a thorough knowledge of the species and its needs.

NCCAW recognises that primates are held as pets, but recommends that the practice be phased out.

People keeping primates should be licensed, subject to their facilities and management skills meeting satisfactory standards, (the standards are similar to those required for primate exhibitors, e.g., circuses).

They should be able to demonstrate their knowledge of the species and its requirements, including diet, welfare, social and behavioural needs and so on. In view of phasing out private ownership of primates, breeding in these situations should be prevented.

Once the present round of licenses has been issued, future licenses will be issued only under exceptional circumstances.

Periodical and Internet Sources Bibliography

The following articles have been selected to supplement the diverse views presented in this chapter.

Kelvin Alie et al.	"Attitudes Towards Dogs and Other 'Pets' in Roseau, Dominica," *Anthrozoos*, vol. 20, no. 2, 2007.
Grace Chua	"Rein in Puppy Mills: Animal Welfare Groups," *Straits Times* (Singapore), July 29, 2010.
Kim Hepple	"We Should Not Turn a Blind Eye to Cruelty," *Hull Daily Mail* (UK), July 28, 2010.
Brendan Howard	"The New Welfare War," *DVM Newsmagazine*, vol. 40, no. 9, September 2009.
Chai Mei Ling	"Taken from Home into a Life of Pain," *New Straits Times* (Malaysia), July 18, 2010.
Tony Milligan	"Dependent Companions," *Journal of Applied Philosophy*, vol. 26, no. 4, November 2009.
Nigel Nelson	"Thugs' Dog Rights May Go Walkies," *People* (London), July 25, 2010.
Megan L. Renwick	"Animal Hoarding: A Legislative Solution," *University of Louisville Law Review*, Winter 2009.
Karen D. Schaefer	"Cruelty to Animals and the Short- and Long-Term Impact on Victims," *Journal of Emotional Abuse*, vol. 7, no. 3, 2007.
Martin C. Wesley, Neresa B. Minatrea, and Joshua C. Watson	"Animal-Assisted Therapy in the Treatment of Substance Dependence," *Anthrozoos*, vol. 22, no. 2, June 2009.
Steven White	"Companion Animals: Members of the Family or Legally Discarded Objects?" *University of New South Wales Law Journal*, vol. 32, no. 3, 2009.

For Further Discussion

Chapter 1

1. The authors in this chapter explore the impact of culture and religion on animal welfare. Do you think culture and religion should be given priority over animal rights? Using the viewpoints in this chapter, explain your answer.

Chapter 2

1. The authors in this chapter debate the treatment of animals in biomedical experiments. Based on these viewpoints, do you think animals are necessary in scientific research? Explain your answer.

Chapter 3

1. After reading the viewpoints in this chapter, do you think animals raised for food are treated humanely? Should they be? Use the viewpoints to back up your answers.

Chapter 4

1. The authors in this chapter discuss the responsibility that human beings have for animals used as companions and helpmates. After reading the viewpoints, do you think companion animals have rights? Explain your answer.

Organizations to Contact

The editors have compiled the following list of organizations concerned with the issues debated in this book. The descriptions are derived from materials provided by the organizations. All have publications or information available for interested readers. The list was compiled on the date of publication of the present volume; the information provided here may change. Be aware that many organizations take several weeks or longer to respond to inquiries, so allow as much time as possible.

American Society for the Prevention of Cruelty to Animals (ASPCA)
424 E. Ninety-Second Street, New York, NY   10128-6804
(212) 876-7700, ext. 4655
e-mail: press@aspca.org
website: www.aspca.org

The American Society for the Prevention of Cruelty to Animals (ASPCA) was founded in 1866 on the belief that animals are entitled to kind and respectful treatment at the hands of humans and must be protected under the law. Headquartered in New York City, the ASPCA maintains a strong local presence; with programs that extend its anticruelty mission across the country, it is recognized as a national animal welfare organization. In addition to links to news reports on animal abuse, the ASPCA's website includes lengthy investigations on animal cruelty across the country.

Animal Aid
The Old Chapel, Bradford Street, Tonbridge, Kent   TN9 1AW
  United Kingdom
+44 (0)1732 364546 • fax: +44 (0)1732 366533
e-mail: info@animalaid.org.uk
website: www.animalaid.org.uk

Established in 1977, Animal Aid is the United Kingdom's largest animal rights group. It promotes a cruelty-free lifestyle and campaigns peacefully against all forms of animal abuse. Animal Aid's undercover investigations are reported on its website along with lessons for teachers to use in the classroom and its monthly e-newsletter.

Animal Defenders International (ADI)

Millbank Tower, Millbank, London   SW1P 4QP
  United Kingdom
+44 (0)20 7630 3340 • fax: +44 (0)20 7828 2179
e-mail: info@ad-international.org
website: www.ad-international.org

Animal Defenders International (ADI) takes a holistic, self-sufficient approach to achieving long-term protection for animals. ADI works at all levels, from start to finish of a campaign—from undercover investigations to scientific and economic research, publication of technical reports, public education, and drafting and securing legislative protection for animals. Background information from all campaigns is available on ADI's website, which also includes articles from its *Annual Review* and *Animal Defenders* magazine.

Animal Legal Defense Fund (ALDF)

170 East Cotati Avenue, Cotati, CA   94931
(707) 795-2533 • fax: (707) 795-7280
e-mail: info@aldf.org
website: www.aldf.org

Founded in 1979 by attorneys active in shaping the emerging field of animal law, Animal Legal Defense Fund (ALDF) has blazed the trail for stronger enforcement of anticruelty laws and more humane treatment of animals in every corner of American life. ALDF works to protect animals by filing lawsuits to stop animal abuse, providing free legal assistance to prosecutors handling cruelty cases, and providing public education through seminars, workshops, and other outreach efforts. In addition to its quarterly newsletter, *The Animals' Advocate*, a number of research reports are available on the ALDF website on such topics as animal protection laws and how to confront animal neglect.

Born Free

3 Grove House, Foundry Lane, Horsham   RH13 5PL
   United Kingdom
e-mail: info@bornfree.org.uk
website: www.bornfree.org.uk

Born Free is an international, nonprofit organization devoted
to halting the race to extinction by protecting rare species in
their natural habitat. Born Free's major international projects
are devoted to animal welfare; conservation and education;
and protection of lions, elephants, gorillas, chimpanzees, tigers, polar bears, wolves, dolphins, turtles, sharks, and other
endangered animals. In addition to annual reports, Born Free's
website provides links to its ongoing campaigns such as animal welfare in zoos, the future of big cats, and ways to protect
at-risk ocean life.

Center for Consumer Freedom

PO Box 34557, Washington, DC   20043
(202) 463-7112
website: www.consumerfreedom.com

The Center for Consumer Freedom is a nonprofit organization dedicated to promoting personal responsibility and protecting consumer choices. The group opposes activists who
meddle in Americans' lives, including proponents of animal
rights, through education and ad campaigns. At the center's
website, one can access print, radio, and TV ads; letters to the
editor; and archived news articles.

Compassion in World Farming (CIWF)

Second Floor, River Court, Mill Lane, Godalming
Surrey   GU7 1EZ
   United Kingdom
+44 (0)1483 521950
e-mail: compassion@ciwf.org.uk
website: www.ciwf.org.uk

Compassion in World Farming (CIWF) was founded in 1967
by a British farmer who became horrified by the development
of modern, intensive factory farming. CIWF continues its ef-

forts to put an end to animal suffering by fighting industrialized farming throughout the world; sponsoring scientific research; conducting undercover investigations; educating the public; and encouraging businesses to sell humanely farmed meat products. In addition to news bulletins, CIWF's website provides a library of research reports, such as "The Role of Factory Farming in the Cause and Spread of Swine Influenza" and "Welfare of Turkeys at Slaughter."

Humane Society of the United States (HSUS)
2100 L Street NW, Washington, DC   20037
(202) 452-1100
e-mail: info@humanesociety.org
website: www.humanesociety.org

Established in 1954, the Humane Society of the United States (HSUS) seeks a humane and sustainable world for all animals. The HSUS works to reduce suffering and to create meaningful social change for animals by advocating for sensible public policies; investigating cruelty; working to enforce existing laws; educating the public about animal issues; joining with corporations on behalf of animal-friendly policies; and conducting hands-on programs that make ours a more humane world. The HSUS website provides links to current news articles about animal welfare along with a large collection of detailed reports on issues such as factory farming and cockfighting.

International Fund for Animal Welfare (IFAW)
290 Summer Street, Yarmouth Port, MA   02675
(800) 932 4329 • fax: (508) 744-2099
e-mail: info@ifaw.org
website: www.ifaw.org

International Fund for Animal Welfare (IFAW) works toward protecting animals worldwide. IFAW raises money and awareness about animal welfare through investigations and campaigns, which have led to the establishment of laws protecting the world's most endangered creatures. In addition to scientific reports, IFAW also publishes *IFAW's Annual Reports* and *World of Animals.*

International Primate Protection League (IPPL)

PO Box 766, Summerville, SC   29484
(843) 871-2280 • fax: (843) 871-7988
e-mail: info@ippl.org
website: www.ippl.org

The International Primate Protection League (IPPL) is a grassroots nonprofit organization dedicated to protecting the world's remaining primates, great and small. IPPL offers advisory and financial support for activities that help monkeys and apes—both in the United States and overseas—publicizes the plight of primates in trouble, organizes international protest campaigns, conducts investigations of illegal international primate trafficking, and operates a sanctuary for rescued gibbon apes in South Carolina. In addition to *IPPL News*, the organization's newsletter, the IPPL website offers an archive of informative annual reports.

People for the Ethical Treatment of Animals (PETA)

501 Front Street, Norfolk, VA   23510
(757) 622-PETA (7382) • fax: (757) 622-0457
e-mail: info@peta.org
website: www.peta.org

People for the Ethical Treatment of Animals (PETA) focuses its attention on the four areas in which the largest numbers of animals suffer the most intensely for the longest periods of time: on factory farms, in laboratories, in the clothing trade, and in the entertainment industry. PETA works through public education, cruelty investigations, research, animal rescue, legislation, special events, celebrity involvement, and protest campaigns. In addition to action alerts and podcasts, PETA's website provides links to feature stories about animal abuse and action campaigns, along with fact sheets on such subjects as companion animals and vegetarianism.

Uncaged Campaigns

5th Floor, Alliance House, 9 Leopold Street
Sheffield S1 2GY
  United Kingdom
+44 (0) 114 272 2220 • fax: +44 (0) 114 272 2225
e-mail: info@uncaged.co.uk
website: www.uncaged.co.uk

Uncaged Campaigns operates at every level, from grassroots protests to motions in Parliament through to participation in academic discourse. Uncaged Campaigns has contributed to numerous government consultation exercises on animal experimentation matters and has given evidence to a recent House of Lords inquiry. Its analysis has appeared in journals and has been quoted by researchers. National and international media have covered Uncaged's work.

Vets Beyond Borders (VBB)

PO Box 576, Crows Nest 1585
  New South Wales
+61 2 9431 8616
website: www.vetsbeyondborders.org

Vets Beyond Borders (VBB), an Australian-based, not-for-profit organization established by veterinary volunteers in 2003, coordinates and runs veterinary-based animal welfare and public health programs in developing communities of the Asian-Pacific region. VBB works with local governments and organizations to establish effective veterinary-based programs; supplies much-needed medications and surgical equipment; facilitates the funding of buildings and important infrastructure such as kennels to hospitalize treated animals; and contributes to the development of wider programs to address animal welfare and community health issues. Along with detailed annual reports, VBB's website includes a document library focused on the ethical care and treatment of animals around the world.

World Society for the Protection of Animals (WSPA)

5th Floor, 222 Grays Inn Road, London   WC1X 8HB
    United Kingdom
+44 (0)20 7239 0500 • fax: +44 (0)20 7239 0653
e-mail: wspa@wspa-international.org
website:www.wspa-international.org

The World Society for the Protection of Animals (WSPA) has been promoting animal welfare for more than twenty-five years and concentrates on regions of the world where few, if any, measures exist to protect animals. WSPA's work is focused on four priority animal welfare areas: companion animals, commercial exploitation of wildlife, farm animals, and disaster management. WSPA offers many resources on its website, including reports on animal abuse, educational materials, and an e-newsletter.

World Wildlife Fund (WWF)

1250 Twenty-Fourth Street NW, PO Box 97180
Washington, DC   20090-7180
(202) 293-4800
website: www.worldwildlife.org

World Wildlife Fund (WWF) is an international organization that seeks to preserve nature and its inhabitants. WWF combines global outreach with a foundation in science, involves action at every level from local to global, and ensures the delivery of innovative solutions that meet the needs of both people and nature. WWF's website includes links to public service announcements, annual reports, and publications such as "Tigers: Will 2010 Be the Last Year of the Tiger?" and "Collaring the Caprivi."

Bibliography of Books

Susan J. Armstrong and Richard G. Botzler, eds. *The Animal Ethics Reader.* New York: Routledge, 2008.

Stephen Aronson *Animal Control Management: A New Look at a Public Responsibility.* West Lafayette, IN: Purdue University Press, 2010.

P. Michael Conn and James V. Parker *The Animal Research War.* New York: Palgrave Macmillan, 2008.

Council of Europe, ed. *Animal Welfare.* Strasbourg, Germany: Council of Europe Publishers, 2006.

Karen Dawn *Thanking the Monkey: Rethinking the Way We Treat Animals.* New York: Harper, 2008.

Rhonda Lucas Donald *Animal Rights: How You Can Make a Difference.* Mankato, MN: Capstone Press, 2009.

David S. Favre *Animal Law: Welfare, Interests, and Rights.* New York: Aspen Publishers, 2008.

David Fraser *Understanding Animal Welfare: The Science in Its Cultural Context.* Ames, IA: Wiley-Blackwell, 2008.

Carrie Gleason *Animal Rights Activist.* New York: Crabtree Publishers, 2010.

Temple Grandin, ed.	*Improving Animal Welfare: A Practical Approach*. Wallingford, Oxfordshire, UK: CAB International, 2010.
Neville G. Gregory	*Animal Welfare and Meat Production*. Wallingford, Oxfordshire, UK: CAB International, 2007.
Mark Hawthorne	*Striking at the Roots: A Practical Guide to Animal Activism*. Washington, DC: O Books, 2008.
Richard P. Haynes	*Animal Welfare: Competing Conceptions and Their Ethical Implications*. New York: Springer, 2010.
Leslie Irvine	*Filling the Ark: Animal Welfare in Disasters*. Philadelphia, PA: Temple University Press, 2009.
Andrew Linzey	*Why Animal Suffering Matters: Philosophy, Theology, and Practical Ethics*. New York: Oxford University Press, 2009.
Andrew Linzey, ed.	*The Link Between Animal Abuse and Human Violence*. Portland, OR: Sussex Academic Press, 2009.
Al-Hafiz Basheer Ahmad Masri	*Animal Welfare in Islam*. Leicestershire, UK: Islamic Foundation, 2007.
David J. Mellor, Emily Patterson-Kane, Kevin J. Stafford	*The Sciences of Animal Welfare*. Ames, IA: Wiley-Blackwell, 2009.

Adrian R.
Morrison
An Odyssey with Animals: A Veterinarian's Reflections on the Animal Rights & Welfare Debate. New York: Oxford University Press, 2009.

Ingrid Newkirk
The PETA Practical Guide to Animal Rights: Simple Acts of Kindness to Help Animals in Trouble. New York: St. Martin's Griffin, 2009.

Clare Palmer, ed.
Animal Rights. Burlington, VT: Ashgate, 2008.

Mark Rowlands
Animal Rights: Moral Theory and Practice. New York: Palgrave Macmillan, 2009.

Peter Sandøe and
Stine B.
Christiansen
Ethics of Animal Use. Oxford, UK: Wiley-Blackwell, 2008.

Kathryn Shevelow
For the Love of Animals: The Rise of the Animal Protection Movement. New York: Henry Holt, 2009.

Wesley J. Smith
A Rat Is a Pig Is a Dog Is a Boy: The Human Cost of the Animal Rights Movement. New York: Encounter Books, 2009.

Erin E. Williams
and Margo
DeMello
Why Animals Matter: The Case for Animal Protection. Amherst, NY: Prometheus Books, 2007.

Index

Geographic headings and page numbers in **boldface** refer to viewpoints about that country or region.

I

J